T0079720

POMEGRANATE

Edible

Series Editor: Andrew F. Smith

EDIBLE is a revolutionary series of books dedicated to food and drink
that explores the rich history of cuisine. Each book reveals the global
history and culture of one type of food or beverage.

Already published

Pomegranate

A Global History

Damien Stone

REAKTION BOOKS

Published by Reaktion Books Ltd
Unit 32, Waterside
44–48 Wharf Road
London N1 7UX, UK
www.reaktionbooks.co.uk

First published 2017

Printed and bound in China by 1010 Printing International Ltd

A catalogue record for this book is available from the British Library

ISBN 978 1 78023 749 7

Contents

Introduction

The pomegranate bush raises its voice (tiny, insistent, and shrill):
'My seeds shine like the teeth of my mistress, the shape of my
fruit is round like her breasts. I'm her favourite, I know, sweetest
tree in the orchard, looking my best through every season.'
Turin Papyrus, Egyptian, 12th century BC

The pomegranate is an unusual, alluring and ornamental fruit.
Even though it can be rather awkward to eat, throughout
human history it has remained a most desirable talismanic food
item. Those who first wrote of the pomegranate, in ancient
Mesopotamia, called it *nurma*, but for us its name derives from
the Latin *pomum* (apple) and *granatum* (seeded). It is from the
fruit's distinctive shape, colour and seeds that its universal
aesthetic appeal originates. The pomegranate embodies beauty,
mystery and the female. Its evocative red juice has often been
likened to blood.

One of the oldest foods in the world, the pomegranate
seems to have come to us originally from the region that
is now modern Iran, wild varieties being born of the bio-
diverse Kopet Dag mountain range. It was first domesticated
during the Neolithic Revolution, which began around 10,000
BC; human selection meant that the pomegranate took on

Pomegranates (*Punica granatum*) for sale, Mysore, India.

appealing qualities it did not have in the wild. The pomegranate makes its first archaeological appearance at the start of the third millennium BC, in the form of carbonized pomegranate seeds excavated at the Middle Eastern sites of Jericho, Arad and Nimrud.[1] In addition to the pomegranate (*Punica granatum*), the genus *Punica* contains one other species. The rare *Punica protopunica* is a precursor from which the common pomegranate may derive. It is found only on the island of Socotra off the coast of Yemen. *P. protopunica* is generally not eaten, however, as it is rather bitter. *Punica* is from the same botanical family as myrtle, the Lythraceae.

The part of the fruit that is of most interest to us is that which is edible: the seeds. Each seed is coated in an aril, that ever-so-desirable, blood-red and juicy, sour-sweet flesh. These are set close together in kaleidoscopic clusters embedded in a yellow or white leathery pulp. The versatility of the fruit, however, extends beyond its culinary function. Its skin, for example, is known to have been used to tan leather. The flowers

Otto Wilhelm Thomé, *Punica granatum*, 19th-century botanical illustration.

of the pomegranate plant can produce a vibrant red dye for use in textiles, while a black dye can be extracted from the plant's roots. From the rind a yellow dye can be made. The pale wood of the pomegranate tree is very hard and durable. However, the small overall dimensions of the tree, with its thin trunk, makes it useless in construction (although an Old Babylonian text does refer to a 3-metre-long pomegranate beam used as a building edifice).[2] Today pomegranate wood is really only used for crafting small-scale agricultural tools and some decorative items. Cups made of pomegranate wood have been made as far back as the Bronze Age.[3]

The pomegranate tree, which is known to live for up to 300 years (although after fifteen years the flavour and production of the fruit declines), is shrub-like in appearance, closely branched and twiggy. Some varieties are evergreen while others are deciduous. The plant usually reaches a maximum height of about 8 metres. It can also be much smaller; dwarf pomegranates are a favourite variety of bonsai in Japan, owing to the plant's ability to achieve a desirable twist in the wood of its trunk, as well as the appeal of its miniature red fruits and flowers. Some pomegranate varieties are fruitless and grown simply for the appeal of their bell-shaped flowers. The pomegranate tree also works well as a hedging plant and has been used to reforest mountain slopes, improving the adverse effects of erosion.

To begin our story, I will make the intimidating pomegranate a little more approachable by explaining the best way to get rid of its off-putting skin and pith, so that the reader can enjoy eating some arils as they discover this fruit's colourful history. When purchasing a fresh pomegranate, note that the optimum fruit has smooth, glossy skin free from cracks and bruises. A pomegranate past its maturity will have dry-looking, wrinkled and tightened skin. There are over a thousand varieties

Pomegranate in growth.

of pomegranate (see Appendix for a selection of these). Although the outer skin is most commonly red, there is a full colour range from dark purple to yellow and green varieties. The inner arils likewise vary in their shade. Sometimes in a single pomegranate, arils of two different colours may be

Pomegranate tree exhibiting its flowers.

found. This is known as metaxenia, and is the result of a plant being fertilized by two different cultivars.

Take your chosen pomegranate and cut off just enough of its crown (known as the calyx) to expose the yellow or white pith. Score the skin downwards in quarters and then allow the fruit to soak in a bowl of cold water for a few minutes. Holding the fruit under water, break it into sections with the fingers, separating the seeds from the pith. The seeds will sink to the bottom of the bowl, while the membrane will float to the top. After discarding the skin, drain the seeds and dry on paper towels. Alternatively, cutting the fruit in half and using a utensil to smack vigorously on the back of the skin will quickly dislodge the arils, although this tends to be a messier method. Your arils are ready for immediate consumption, and for use in cooking. Alternatively, they will last for up to one month in the refrigerator, or about three months in the freezer. Many people enjoy the juicy pulp of the aril but do not like consuming the central seed itself. To juice your fruit, you can use a blender to process the arils, afterwards using cheesecloth to separate the desired liquid from the leftover solids. Otherwise the pomegranate can be cut in half and have its juices squeezed out by means of a citrus press. When the juice is boiled it becomes concentrated, eventually developing into a thick, dark molasses.

I

The Primordial Pomegranate: The Fruit in Myth

But secretly he slipped into my mouth a seed from
a pomegranate, that honey-sweet food, and forced me,
made me taste it against my will.
Homeric hymn to Demeter, 7th–6th century BC

Ancient Greece

Our story begins in the timeless realm of myth, through which
people inspired by the pomegranate have composed fantastical
accounts featuring the fruit. The pomegranate came to be
an important figure in the literary lore passed down in both
Eastern and Western cultures. Acting as a symbol of fecundity
in both traditions, the pomegranate shows the dual nature of
fertility, sometimes offering life, but also bringing about death.

The quotation at the beginning of this chapter is from
one of the best-known stories about the pomegranate that
comes to us from the classical world. This myth revolves around
Persephone, the daughter of the Greek goddess of agriculture,
Demeter. Persephone is kidnapped by Hades, the god of the
dead, and taken to the underworld to be his wife and queen.

Demeter, overwrought by her daughter's untimely descent into the land of the dead, renders the earth barren, destroying all of its vegetation. This in turn causes mankind to starve, and thus Zeus intervenes and demands that Hades return Persephone. Hades, unwilling to give up his new bride completely, tempts her with some pomegranate seeds. Although Persephone is released, because she tasted the food of the underworld, she is required to spend a third of each year there. She is permitted to spend the rest of the year with the other gods above. This myth was used by its classical audience as an explanation for the changing of the seasons: the portion of the year when Persephone was absent was winter, when Demeter once again stripped the earth of life and went into mourning. Persephone's resurrection came in the springtime, marked by rebirth in the natural world.

A mystery religion devoted to Demeter and her daughter, centred on the site of Eleusis in Attica, seems to have promoted the idea of a pleasant existence after death for initiates. Ancient sources are quiet about what secret rituals occurred there, but it is speculated that a re-enactment of the myth took place, which probably required initiates to eat or drink from a pomegranate. The pomegranate in the Persephone myth symbolizes female fertility, as well as the loss of virginity that comes with the consummation of marriage, evoked by both its red stains and its rich seeds. Imagery of the fruit functions as a reminder of what it is to be a woman, the red seeds that spill from the pomegranate replicating the blood of the menstrual cycle. Greek medicine in fact prescribed pomegranate juice as a way of stopping menstrual bleeding.[1]

The woman's monthly bleeding was seen as her equivalent of the man's fighting on the battlefield as a warrior, and thus the pomegranate was an attribute of the martial virgin goddess Athena, the protectress of young Athenian girls of a marriageable age. The Temple of Athena Nike atop the Acropolis housed a wooden cult statue that has long since been lost to decay, which depicted Athena with a pomegranate in her right hand (signifying the female battle), and a helmet in her left (the male battle).[2]

Athena is likewise represented with the pomegranate on several different ancient coins from Side in Pamphylia (on the southern Mediterranean coast of what is now Turkey). As well as giving its name to a place, *side* is one of the ancient Greek words for pomegranate, and was also personified as the name of the wife of Orion. It is thought that the wedding of Orion to Side is a mythological explanation for the ripening of autumnal fruit, which occurs during the time of year when the Orion constellation can be seen in the night sky. Not all goes well for the happy couple, however, as Side commits a grave act of arrogance, comparing her ornamental beauty with that of the queen of the gods, Hera. Side, for punishment, is sent to the underworld for eternity, hence the association between the pomegranate and that place. Another tradition refers to Side as a young virgin who commits suicide on her mother's grave in order to avoid being raped by her father. Her blood gives birth to a pomegranate tree.

As a result of Hera's involvement in the myth of Side, she is often represented holding a pomegranate. One such representation was created by the sculptural master Polykleitos at Argos in the fifth century BC. Being made of ivory and gold, the sculpture did not survive antiquity, but sources tell us that in one of her hands Hera held a pomegranate as a globus cruciger. Pausanias, who saw the chryselephantine statue, writes: 'About the pomegranate I must say nothing, for its story is somewhat of a holy mystery.'[3] This suggests that there existed a secret cult to Hera, requiring initiation, which revolved around the pomegranate, probably in connection with the Hera and Side myth. An important sanctuary to Hera is located in southern Italy at the Greek settlement of Paestum, where a chapel now stands to Madonna del Granato (Our Lady of the Pomegranate). The archaeologist Helmut Kyrieleis has noted that Mary, 'by virtue of her epithet and the attribute of a pomegranate must be the Christian successor of the ancient Greek goddess Hera'.[4] The pomegranate that emphasized the fertility and domestic role of the ancient Greek mother of the gods thus came to be adopted by the virgin mother of the Christian God.

But the pomegranate in Greek myth wasn't just a symbol of fertility in the feminine sense. In ancient Greek society, a woman's body was traditionally seen as an empty vessel that needed to be filled by a man. A son was said to be a closer blood relation to his father, who planted his seed, than to his mother, who is simply the soil in which it was sown.[5] Thus it was appropriate that the creation of the pomegranate plant, with its ever-fertile seeds, should be explained in masculine terms. The first pomegranate was consequently said to have been created by Aphrodite from the blood of her dying mortal lover Adonis.[6] The fruit was one of the symbols of the sexually powerful Aphrodite, the goddess said to have first planted the pomegranate on the island of Cyprus. The fruit is often linked with depictions of Aphrodite, as on an Etruscan bronze mirror of 300 BC engraved with an image of the goddess holding a pomegranate-topped sceptre. The depiction of immortal figures on Etruscan mirrors is common, and an individual who used such a mirror would see the divine image of perfection imposed over his/her own reflection.

Adonis was not the only male figure from whose blood the pomegranate was perceived to have resulted. The same motif appeared in the myth surrounding the Phrygian great mother goddess, Cybele. Cybele is thought to derive from an earlier Hittite goddess named Kubaba, who in representations

Hittite goddess Kubaba holding a pomegranate, 9th–8th century BC.

from the ninth to eight century BC is shown holding a pomegranate in one of her hands and a mirror in the other. Her tale
begins with the birth of a wild man named Agdestis, who
wreaks havoc among gods and mortals alike. The god of wine,
Dionysus, decides to intervene and spikes the water fountain
where Agdestis comes to drink. A drunken Agdestis falls into

slumber, after which Dionysus uses a rope to bind his feet and makes a vine grow over his genitals. When Agdestis arises, stumbling to his feet in his hungover state, his genitals are ripped from his body by the entwined plant. From the blood that is spilled from his groin (replicating semen) onto the earth, a pomegranate tree grows. The story continues that a river nymph named Nana eats one of the pomegranates from the tree. Ripe with bloody seeds, the fruit in turn impregnates her. She gives birth to Attis, who then becomes Cybele's lover. Throughout this bizarre myth, the pomegranate is the generative and transformative force, literally taking the role of the man in procreation.

Although grapes are the main attribute of the god of wine, Dionysus, the pomegranate is also associated with him in a number of myths. In a tale of his infancy, he is torn up and eaten by the Titans (though later reassembled). From the blood that spills onto the earth as he is cannibalized, a pomegranate tree grows. Thus certain ritual festivals banned the consumption of the pomegranate as being too sacred. Clement of Alexandria tells us: 'The women who celebrate the Thesmophoria are careful not to eat any pomegranate seeds which fall to the ground, being of opinion that pomegranates spring from the drops of Dionysus' blood.'[7] Later, as an adult god, Dionysus seduces a maiden under the pretence that he will give her a crown. When she badgers the god for her reward, he turns her into a pomegranate, with its crown-shaped calyx.

Two final incidents in classical myth that allude to the pomegranate have the fruit as the catalyst for great suffering. The first concerns Tantalus, a mortal figure punished by the gods to suffer an eternal torment in the underworld. His name is the source of the English word 'tantalize'. Tantalus was forced to stand in a pool of water beneath a fruit tree with low branches, with the fruit ever eluding his grasp, and the water always receding before he could take a drink. Different sources depict him reaching out for different fruit; some (Homer's *Odyssey* included) appropriately choose the pomegranate, the plentiful seeds of the desired fruit contrasting with Tantalus' torment of emptiness that makes him hunger and thirst eternally in the underworld. The other myth that contains a fruit which can be interpreted as a pomegranate is that of the Judgement of Paris. The story goes that in a beauty competition between the Greek goddesses, the Trojan prince, Paris, awards Aphrodite a prized 'golden apple', that is, a pomegranate.[8] The ancient Greek word for apple, *mêlon*, was also sometimes used to describe pomegranates, which were much more common in the Mediterranean. The pomegranate, after all, was one of Aphrodite's attributes, as well as being associated with both Athena and Hera, who also vied for the fruit in the competition. The pomegranate was considered an aphrodisiac with magical properties, and thus, for Paris, the fruit allows for the wish-fulfilment of gaining Helen, the most beautiful woman in the world. Paris awards the fruit to Aphrodite after she offers him Helen, wife of the king of Sparta. Helen's abduction inevitably causes conflict. The fateful fruit, inscribed with the words *Ti Kallisti* (For the Fairest), thus becomes responsible for the start of the Trojan War. The pomegranate's red, spilling seeds appropriately forecast the bloodshed that will result.

Arabia, Persia and Turkey

Centuries later, another literary tradition that was similarly obsessed with the pomegranate developed in the Middle East. Under an Islamic backdrop, the pomegranate remains sexually charged.

Limestone hand clutching a pomegranate, all that survives from a large Cypriot statue, 6th century BC.

The One Thousand and One Nights is an anthology of many tales from Arabian folklore, structured within the framework of the story of Scheherazade, who uses her ability as a storyteller to avoid execution. The pomegranate appears in many of her tales. One story concerns the son of the king of Yemen, Sayf, who on his adventures meets a man without arms and legs who has been fed pomegranate seeds by mice for 700 years while he waited for the prince's arrival. This link between the pomegranate and the infinite is also found in another tale relating to Hayid, a prophet to whom God grants a pomegranate with an unending amount of arils that will feed him perpetually. The 'Tale of the Young Nur and the Warrior Girl' contains several short songs in praise of various fruits.

The hymn relating to the pomegranate compares the fruit's shape to the alluring female form:

> Polished delicates are we,
> Ruby mines in silver earth,
> Maidens' blood of high degree
> Curdled into drops of worth,
> Breasts of women when they see
> Man is near, and stand them forth.[9]

A very fertile pomegranate occurs in an Arabian Nights tale revolving around the sultan of Diyarbakr. The story begins by noting the sultan's inability to produce any children. He has a dream in which he is told to go to his garden and request a pomegranate from his gardener. He does as the dream commands. The Sultan eats fifty seeds from the pomegranate he is given and promptly all fifty of his wives become pregnant. One of the concubines, a woman named Pirouze, does not appear at first to be with child, and is sent away, but is later discovered to be pregnant anyway.

Another transformative pomegranate is to be found in the 'Twelfth Captain's Tale'. Our hero is a prince by the name of Muhammad who comes up against an evil sorcerer Moor. Muhammad is able to escape and overcome the Moor by transfiguring into a pomegranate:

> To escape his persecutor, the prince used the virtue of the cord to change into a large pomegranate . . . as soon as the Moor touched it, it burst asunder, and all the grains were scattered on the floor. The sorcerer picked them up, one by one, until he came to the last grain . . . which contained the vital essence of Muhammad. As the vile magician stretched out his neck towards this final grain,

a dagger came up out of it and stabbed him to the heart, so that he spat out his unbelieving soul in a stream of blood.[10]

The blow to the Moor is fatal, the blood-evoking pomegranate bringing about his bloody end.

The Shahnameh, Iran's national epic by the poet Ferdowsi, narrates the lives of the Persian kings from the beginning of time until the seventh century AD. It is a conglomeration of a vast amount of mythology, legend and history that includes among its tales several references to the pomegranate. The fruit is used in a description of the physical beauty that first attracts the warrior Zal to his future wife Rudabeh: 'Her mouth resembles a pomegranate blossom, her lips are cherries and her silver bosom curves out into breasts like pomegranates.'[11] Zal and Rudabeh have a son, the great Persian hero Rostam. Rostam would eventually take up arms against another Persian hero, Esfandiyar, who had previously been rendered invincible from eating a pomegranate. Esfandiyar, however, like Achilles, has one vulnerable spot: his eyes. The pomegranate's power cannot defend him from an arrow from Rostam's bow, shot straight through Esfandiyar's pupil. The Shahnameh again associates the fruit with death following the beheading of Siavash. The text notes how the pomegranate trees of the forest withered in sorrow after the wrongful execution of the Iranian hero.

One final story of the pomegranate in the Persian epic concerns a man named Farhad who becomes the lover of King Khosrow's wife, Shirin. As punishment for his transgression, he is exiled to Mount Behistun (known to us for its famed inscription by Darius the Great, which was later the key to the decipherment of cuneiform in the nineteenth century). He is given the task of clearing away the mountain with an axe, and told that if he successfully finds water he will be allowed to marry Shirin. Many years go by. It is not until Farhad has removed half the mountain that he does in fact find water. Khosrow approaches him with the (false) news that Shirin has died. Farhad goes mad with grief, throws his axe down and dies. Where the thrown axe falls, a pomegranate tree grows that bears fruit with the power to cure sickness.

In a fairy tale from Turkey, the son of a king desires a certain princess. After completing several challenges set by her father in order to gain an audience with the princess, she sets the youth a task herself: to retrieve a singing pomegranate branch from the Garden of Reh-Dew. Facing adversity along the way, the prince finally arrives at the garden and sees the pomegranates hanging from a tree like lamps. He picks off a branch with some fifty pomegranates on it, 'each of which sang a different song, as though all the music of the world were brought together there'.[12] On retrieving the branch he is told by the guardian of the garden: 'never let it out of your sight. If you can listen to it throughout your wedding day the pomegranates will love you; you need fear nothing, for they will protect you in any distress.'[13] The princess becomes aware of her champion's return when she hears the many tunes of the fifty fruits echoing through her city. As she meets the prince, 'the pomegranate branch chanted the union of their two hearts in such exquisite strains that they seemed to be lifted up from this earth to the Paradise of Allah.'[14] Throughout their lengthy forty-day wedding, the couple continuously listen to the singing of the pomegranates. An imposter prince tries to claim the princess for himself, but the sound of the pomegranates that the prince and princess heard during their wedding keeps evil at bay. Although the true prince is beheaded, he is restored back to life and the pretender is overcome. In this tale, the princess's requirement for her suitor to retrieve the pomegranate branch is most interesting. As the branch has the power to guarantee a positive marriage experience, it functions like a dowry and alleviates the uncertainty that comes with being a bride. In traditional Turkish culture (and in other parts of this region, such as Armenia and Iran) the pomegranate is associated with weddings. Following the service, a bride may choose to toss a pomegranate on the floor. The number of seeds that spill out of the fruit are playfully considered to indicate the number of children she will have. Surely a choir of fifty pomegranates would grant the prince and princess an abundance of children.

The pomegranate occurs alongside this literary motif of the suitor's challenge in another fairy tale known as 'The Parrot Shah'. The story relates that an overprotective father makes use of a pomegranate to protect his daughter:

> The king was very possessive and wanted to keep Gala all to himself, and with the help of a wizard, he had thought up a plan to discourage her suitors. A magic tree was planted in the garden, a huge pomegranate that had three fruits. At sunset, the branches bent over to touch the ground and the fruit split open. Inside each lay a soft feather bed. Gala, the princess, slept in the middle one, with her servants on each side. The fruit closed over the maidens and the branches swung back to the sky, carrying the princess high above all danger. Seven walls were built round the garden, each studded with thousands of spikes which nobody could ever cross.[15]

The challenge of wooing the princess is eventually achieved by a shah of distant Persia who is able to transmigrate into the body of a parrot and fly off with the pomegranate. The sexual implications of the imagery in this tale are implicit.

The desirable virgin, lying on a bed inside a red and seeded fruit, represents one thing for a man: sexual potential. The father's attempt to use a feminine fruit, which splits open and closes up again, to obstruct masculine advances on his daughter makes her all the more enticing. A similar story is found in the beginning of the Persian legend surrounding the Simurgh bird:

> In the garden of the palace there grew a pomegranate tree with only three pomegranates; their seeds were fabulous gems that shone like lamps by night. When ripe, the pomegranates would turn into three beautiful girls who were to become the wives of the three princes.[16]

The pomegranates are likewise stolen, only this time by a malevolent hand that descends from a dark cloud.

2

Pomegranates in the Ancient World

If he is in his seventies and gasping respiration continually afflicts him and he asks for pomegranates, he will die. If he is in his seventies and he asks for dates and eats them, he will get well.

Mesopotamian omen-based medical text, 9th–7th century BC

The Ancient Near East: Mesopotamia, Egypt and Persia

History begins with the invention of writing in Iraq in the late fourth millennium BC, and with it the history of the pomegranate. The creation of writing developed alongside the practice of marking possessions with seals. One Mesopotamian individual living in the first cities around 3500–3000 BC chose the motif of a pomegranate to mark ownership of property. Complete with engravings schematically representing the internal sections of the fruit, the seal is one of the earliest surviving artistic representations of a pomegranate. This seal would have functioned as a form of identification, acting as a personal signature on accounting/trade documents written in clay, and ensuring the security of valued commodities sealed in vessels. The seal has perforations so that it could be worn

Mesopotamian stamp seal and its impression in the form of a pomegranate, 3500–3000 BC.

on the body, either around the neck or on the wrist, as an item of jewellery. This steatite pomegranate was therefore inseparable from its owner's identity, embodying who they were. The fruit was probably chosen as the icon for a seal for its symbolic value. This pomegranate, stamped on daily business transactions, evoked the fruit's fertility, guaranteeing its owner fruitfulness in his affairs.

A roughly contemporary artefact, an alabaster vessel known as the Uruk Vase, represents the levels of world order during this time. The temple, the plain on which divine and human interaction occurs, is represented in the topmost register. Underneath this a register bears a representation of the world of man. Further down is a register of domesticated animals. Out of the watery bottom layer, trees grow, some of which bear a trio of pomegranates. The pomegranate is among the vegetal base on which society rests, enjoyed by the upper human and divine realms.

Although it is fortunate that recipes survive from ancient Mesopotamia, they are quiet as regards to the pomegranate's use in cooking. The fruit seems to have been a popular banquet item, one text recording the serving at a wedding of 'large pomegranate seeds plucked from their rinds'. Another manuscript notes that a hundred pomegranates were served as condiments among a long list of foods served at a feast held by the Assyrian king Ashurnasirpal II.[1] Cuneiform tablets indicate that pomegranate was one of the various flavours added to the national and staple beverage invented by the Mesopotamian people: beer.

The pomegranate also makes an appearance in Mesopotamian narratives. Sumerian literature is dripping with plant- and agricultural-based allegories representing sexual intercourse. The pomegranate fits well among these. In one composition the historic king Shulgi (2094–2047 BC) approaches Inanna (also known as Ishtar), the Sumerian goddess of sex and war, with the following proposition: 'My sister, I would go with you to my pomegranate-tree. I would plant there my sweet, honey covered . . . '.[2] A break in the text leaves it up to our imagination as to just how Shulgi spills the seed and juice of his pomegranate on the goddess. The Old Testament draws directly from this Near Eastern tradition, for the author of the Song of Songs (7:2) likewise exclaims: 'Let us go forth into the fields . . . where the pomegranates are in bloom. There I will give you my love.' The suggestiveness continues throughout this book: 'I would give you spiced wine to drink, the juice of my pomegranate (Songs 8:2).' Even later in Mesopotamia, during the Assyrian period of the first millennium BC, the fruit remains explicitly sexualized in texts. An incantation text of the period thus reads:

Incantation: A maid, beautiful, loving, has come forth. The goddess Ishtar, who loveth the apple and pomegranate, sexual strength, has come forth.

Prayer for: If a woman has raised her eye to a man's penis.

Ritual for it: Recite the incantation three times over either an apple or a pomegranate. Give it to the woman. Make her suck its juice. That woman will come and he will love her.[3]

This is imitative magic, drawing on the fertile juice of the apple/pomegranate in order to bring forth bodily fluids. Throughout the Mesopotamian textual tradition the fruit has strong ties with divinity, one Assyrian tablet describing a deity whose knees are pomegranates.[4] It is represented as literally part of a god. The strong link between the pomegranate and Inanna/Ishtar would influence the classical construction of female divinity.

Iconographically, the pomegranate is relatively rare in ancient Mesopotamian art. It does not occur in any sexualized images; rather, the fruit's powers are drawn upon in the more tranquil setting of the scenes featuring the Assyrian Tree of Life. This motif features on large-scale palatial reliefs as well as smaller decorative seals and ivories. The plant species that this tree is supposed to represent has long been debated over in scholarly circles (it is usually thought to be the date palm). Occasionally, however, the standard palmettes that are characteristic of representations of the sacred tree are replaced, undeniably so by pomegranates. Sometimes, the winged genii (known as *Apkallu*) who heraldically approach the tree in procession are also represented carrying a pomegranate branch. The pomegranate probably served an apotropaic function, absorbing the evil that might otherwise possess the human inhabitants of the palace, as well as representing the Assyrian empire as a fruitful garden through its connotations with fertility.

Meanwhile, in Egypt, the pomegranate is remarkably absent from the Nile Valley region until the beginning of the

Egyptian
ointment spoon,
1336–1327 BC.

Assyrian cylinder seal and its impression illustrating the Assyrian sacred
tree with pomegranates (replacing the standard palmettes), 850–825 BC.
The king is represented symmetrically on both sides of the sacred tree,
with two winged guardians behind him. The chief Assyrian god, Asshur,
floats above the scene.

New Kingdom period (sixteenth to eleventh century BC). By this time we have evidence for ancient intercontinental trade, or perhaps royal gift-giving, of the fruit, as attested by the presence of whole pomegranates found aboard the Ulu Burun shipwreck, a merchant vessel that sank with its vast international assemblage of cargo in the Mediterranean during the fourteenth century BC. A bronze cultic tripod of this period from Ugarit, Syria, is decorated with hanging pomegranate pendants, emphasizing the association the fruit had come to have across the ancient world with ritual, sacrifice and offering. The fruit was probably first brought back to Egypt as booty from the military conquests in Palestine and Syria that characterized the Egyptian experience of the early Eighteenth Dynasty. The pomegranate became a refreshing feature of Egyptian gardens, and, as highlighted in the quote from the Turin Papyrus featured in the Introduction, influenced

Amarna relief depicting Nefertiti sitting on Akhenaten's lap and holding one of his daughters, 14th century BC. In front of the royal family is a container filled with fruit, including pomegranates.

the Egyptian concept of beauty. The pomegranate is included among the remedies of one of the oldest medical compilations, the Egyptian Papyrus Ebers of the sixteenth century BC, which suggests that it can be used as a treatment for the management of tapeworms. The pomegranate would have been quite effective against tapeworms, as its high alkaline value would paralyse the parasite's nervous system.

The pomegranate appears in Egyptian art in both monumental temple reliefs and smaller, personal items. The Brooklyn Museum houses a colourful pomegranate-inspired ivory ointment spoon. The bowl of the ornamental spoon is crafted in the form of a large yellow-brown pomegranate. A second identical pomegranate covers the spoon bowl, acting as a lid that is slid open and closed by means of a pivot. Flowers, leaves and smaller pomegranates jut out from the stem that functions as the handle. The spoon demonstrates the Egyptian tendency to stylize the natural. The artisan who made it probably never saw a pomegranate tree in growth, for what is represented is an ideal rather than a reality: flowers and fruit never appear on the pomegranate plant at the same time. Even in Tutankhamun's famed tomb we find a representation of the fruit: a silver pomegranate-shaped repoussé vessel. Such a vessel may have contained pomegranate juice. As in Mesopotamia, the juice was added to alcoholic beverages, although in Egypt a myth gave new significance to the pomegranate-beer cocktail: it was responsible for saving mankind. The tale tells us that the lion goddess Sekhmet, who has a taste for human blood, plans the mass destruction of all humanity. She is stopped by the sun god Re, who floods her path with a mixture of beer and pomegranate juice poured from 7,000 jugs. Sekhmet mistakes the red liquid for blood and quickly drinks it all. She is thus too drunk to pursue her slaughter. The pomegranate-shaped vases, charms and dried fruit specimens

Hellenistic terracotta stamp seal from Egypt, illustrating a pomegranate in the centre of a basket composition, 2nd–1st century BC.

that have been found in many Egyptian burials were probably placed there as a symbol of the anticipated rebirth of the deceased into the afterlife. The fruit had ensured the survival of mankind once already in life, so why not in death?

From 550–330 BC, Egypt, Mesopotamia and the rest of the ancient Near East had come under the control of the Persian Empire. A cuneiform document from the Metropolitan Museum of Art records a Persian account of a rent payment made in pomegranates, attesting to their continued value and desirability. The Persian king Darius the Great is represented holding a pomegranate flower in a religious ritual at his capital of Persepolis. Alexander the Great would of course defeat the Persian Empire and absorb all this territory as his own; following his untimely death in his early thirties it was divided among his generals. Marking property was still practised at this time, with a stamp seal from Ptolemaic Egypt demonstrating the continued use of a pomegranate motif, although one that is much more elaborate, some 3,000 years later.

Following this period of Greek rule, a second Persian empire arose in Iran, that of the Parthians (247 BC–AD 224). The pomegranate features prominently on the decorative programme of their capital, Ctesiphon. The later Sassanian (AD 224–651) site of Nizamabad depicts rows of pomegranates with wings in relief, a style that would influence Islamic designs. Numerous silver plates that survive from this period depict the exploits of the Sassanian kings. One of these features the pomegranate between a pair of rams' horns worn by a queen in what appears to be a marriage scene. She receives the ring

Silver pomegranate vase from Tutankhamun's tomb, 14th century BC.

Frieze from Nizamabad featuring winged pomegranates, 7th century AD.

Sassanian silver plate, 6–7th century AD.

of rulership from the king, who wears a pine-cone-topped crown equally evocative of fertility. Zoroastrianism was the religion of all these Persian kings, and its temples were traditionally surrounded by pomegranate trees. This religion is still practised today, and involves use of the pomegranate in certain rituals. The initiate of a Navjote, the Zoroastrian coming of age ceremony, is asked to sip a consecrated liquid known as *nirang* in order to cleanse both body and soul. Traditionally this drink was the urine of a virile bull, but pomegranate juice is used as a substitute today. Celebration of *Nowruz*, the Persian New Year, involves the presentation of a bowl of water containing a pomegranate into which coins have been inserted, or sometimes just a single pomegranate twig is used. The coin-encrusted fruit acts as a symbol for prosperity, longevity and good health. All these modern Iranian practices had their roots in the ancient Persian empires.

The Classical World

There are only a few examples of the representation of pomegranates in the Bronze Age Aegean cultures of the Minoans and Mycenaeans. There is a similarity of shape between the pomegranate and the opium poppy, both plants having ancient connotations of fertility. There is no reason why the 'opium' crown of the Minoan 'poppy goddess' cannot be interpreted as a pomegranate. It is not until the advent of the Geometric period in Greece that we start to see a real explosion of clear material evidence relating to the pomegranate.

From the tenth to eighth century BC a type of pomegranate-shaped vase was particularly prevalent, covered in geometric motifs: zigzags, triangles, meanders, swastikas, chequering. Undecorated ceramic pomegranates have likewise been found in the Levant from this period. The redness of the clay is effective in representing the fruit. The Geometric Greek vessels are wheel-made and have a small hole in the bottom, allowing liquid libations to be poured through them, or pebbles to be inserted to enable use as a rattle. This period was the time in Greece when myths started to be written down. The nature of the pomegranate came to define the powers of the gods in these stories. The fruit's ornamental form associated it with the beauty of Aphrodite. The likeness of pomegranate juice to blood represented life and death in the cult of Persephone. The abundance of seeds made it an appropriate symbol for marriage, presided over by the mother goddess Hera.[5] Votive clay pomegranates as well as real fruits were left as offerings at tombs (possibly hung from the calyx), as well as the various sanctuaries of these divine figures. The pomegranate vessel, which died out after the Geometric Period, may have influenced the form of the standard *aryballos*, a small spherical flask with a narrow neck used for holding perfume or oil.

A rather unusual ceramic that features the pomegranate is a *kernos* found at the temple of Hera at Samos. This unusual vessel of the sixth century BC is made up of a hollow circular tube affixed to smaller pots of various shapes that feed into it. These small vessels include the form of the pomegranate, standing out as the sole plant item, among both animal (such as a bull, shellfish, a toad and a ram) and human (a male warrior and a domestic female) shapes. The *kernos* seems to have developed from an even older Near Eastern form: other examples of this type of vessel, although much less sophisticated (having only three feeder vessels: a pomegranate, a bull and a bird), have been excavated from sites such as the ninth-century BC Levant settlement of Tel es-Safi. The general theme seems to be one of plenty and the circular shape suggests that the whole ceramic is a representation of world order. The vessel

Terracotta vase from Attica in the form of a pomegranate, 8th century BC.

may have been used to mix ritual liquids and grains, each being poured through the smaller vessel that functioned as a symbol for that ingredient, the strange cocktail being shared as a drink between individuals from the cup-shaped attachments. In the pomegranate vessel's case, the sacred juice of the fruit is a likely candidate.

Classical vase painting frequently places the pomegranate in scenes of a funerary nature (it should be remembered that most Greek vases of which the whole vessel survives are from funerary contexts, since they were buried as offerings with the

Kernos from the Heraion of Samos, 7th century BC.

Kernos from Tel es-Safi, 9th century BC.

dead). A red-figure *pelike* illustrates the mythological figure Electra mourning at the tomb of her father Agamemnon, in front of which several offering items have been placed, including a pomegranate. In another vase scene, a figure in armour is being handed a pomegranate, the fruit reflecting the bloodiness he faces on the battlefield. The warrior, however, holds up his right hand in a gesture that seems to be declining the offered fruit, as if refusing to accept death.

It is not only death, however, that is represented on vase illustrations featuring pomegranates. Other scenes portray women performing domestic and ritual tasks, such as wedding preparation. The pomegranate will often be depicted placed between individuals of the opposite sex as they gaze at each other, as if for the first time. Several vase paintings depict the winged god Eros with a pomegranate, linking the fruit with the personification of desire itself. The fruit also features commonly as a stylistic border decoration on vases.

In emotive grave stele from Greek cemeteries, the dead are either represented solo in a contemplative stance or saying goodbye to their living loved ones, who lose composure as they reach out, unwilling to let go. Both male and female dead are often depicted holding pomegranates. Examples of this include the stele of a certain Polyxena and of Megakles. On the fifth-century BC Harpy Tomb of Xanthus in Turkey, one frieze represents a procession of women towards a seated female who holds a pomegranate in one hand and a pomegranate flower in the other, which she raises to her nose. Each of the women holds various attributes. One of them carries the same fruit and flower as the seated woman. While the seated figure may be a deity, it is more likely that this is an heroic representation of an individual who was buried in the tomb being brought offerings by her living family members. The strong association between the pomegranate and such scenes

Red-figure *pelike*, 4th century BC. To the right of the mourning Electra, a pomegranate sits on her father's grave.

Black-figure amphora, 6th century BC. A warrior declines the offering of a pomegranate.

of death suggests that the fruit was considered a chthonic symbol, which would ensure safe transition to the underworld for the deceased. After all, Persephone was restored to life for at least some of the year.

In a rare example of surviving Greek fresco paintings from the Lucanian tombs at Paestum, depictions of large red pomegranates are found in abundance. They hang rather conspicuously above a variety of scenes: the laying out of the dead body, people mourning the deceased, women doing textile work, agricultural labour, chariot racing, hunting, warriors in combat, banqueting and images of mythical creatures. The pomegranate fits well among the funerary rite scenes, but what of the domestic activities and sporting contests? The pomegranate may be physical, literally hung during the period of mourning, funerary games and feasts in memory of the deceased. Or it may be a symbol, repeated throughout this variety of different scenes, that hints at a belief in the promise of a continued pleasant existence after death. The fruit demarcates not real-world events, but heroic activities performed in the underworld, the pomegranate being the one constant that guides the deceased through these pursuits. It is likewise found elsewhere in Italian tomb painting, in the even older Etruscan cemetery at Cerveteri, where branches of the fruit held by women feature on decorative plaques.

Several ancient Greek writers describe tombs on which the pomegranate grows of its own accord, as a living memorial of the dead buried there. Pausanias writes of how a pomegranate plant germinated on the tomb of the hero Menoikeus, who, according to legend, killed himself to fulfil a prophecy

West frieze from the Harpy Tomb of Xanthus, Turkey, 5th century BC. Note that two other individuals on the south (a male) and east (a female) sides of the tomb likewise hold pomegranates.

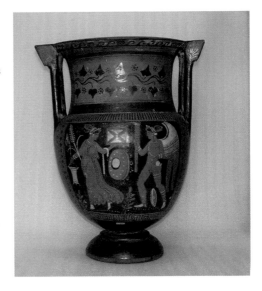

Red-figure column krater, 4th century BC. Eros, wearing a pomegranate on his hip, approaches a woman.

that guaranteed the survival of the city of Thebes at the price of his life.[6] The bloody interior of the fruit reflects his self-sacrifice that saved the city. The same phenomenon occurred at the graves of two other individuals buried at Thebes, one of whom died defending the city, the other while attacking it. These were the brothers Eteokles and Polyneikes, who killed each other in combat.[7] The Furies planted pomegranate plants on their tombs, which Philostratus' *Images* tells us had split-open fruits that were forever dripping blood. The pomegranate is used to imbue real physical spaces with a mythic tradition.

Pomegranates feature in ancient Greek sculpture, largely in that civilization's Archaic period (eighth century BC to 480 BC), when they often appear held by kore statues. These statues portray young women with a braided hairstyle wearing heavy drapery. They are most commonly found in a sanctuary context. Kore statues typically hold an offering of either a flower, a fruit or a bird. Several examples hold a pomegranate: the

Detail of Lucanian tomb painting showing a pomegranate and dog.

notable Berlin Kore, for instance, is represented holding the fruit turned on its side with its calyx facing the viewer. Kore statues acted as an advertisement, to display and celebrate a family's daughter under the guise of a dedication to the gods. These sculptures were not portraits but the ideal. Indicating a girl's eligibility for marriage, they were used as vehicles for the creation of alliances with other elite families. The attribute of a pomegranate would accentuate her beauty and desirability. Like most sculpture from the classical world, these would originally have been painted vibrant colours. Red pigment poignantly survives on a pomegranate held to the breast of a now headless kore statue, Acr. 593, from the Athenian

Acropolis. The kore statues were also sometimes used as grave markers. It is plausible that those of these statues that hold pomegranates indicate a girl who died young, portraying her in the likeness of Persephone. A kore portraying a girl named Phrasikleia holds out a single pomegranate aril and wears a necklace with beads shaped like the fruit. A heart-wrenching inscription on the statue reflects that she died before she

Lucanian tomb painting depicting a victorious warrior surrounded by floating pomegranates, 5th century BC.

had the opportunity to bear fruit: 'Grave marker of Phrasikleia. I shall be called a maiden forever, having been allotted this name by the gods in place of marriage.'[8]

However, it was not only female statues that held pomegranates. The famed ancient Greek wrestler Milo of Croton had a statue of himself holding a pomegranate set up at Olympia.[9] This was a reflection of Milo's position as a priest of Hera, and of a legend circulating about the wrestler that he was able to hold a pomegranate without it splitting open while competitors tried to pry it from his fingers.

Homer recounts in the *Odyssey* that the legendary eastern king Alcinous grew pomegranates in his garden.[10] This is the beginning of a preoccupation in the accounts of ancient Greek writers with representing the East, several making use of a pomegranate in their construction of the non-Greek Other. These ancient historians saw Eastern luxury as decadent and effeminate, assuming that soft countries breed soft men. The father of history, Herodotus, tells us that the famous 10,000 'Immortals' of the Persian army (the unit's name stemming from the custom that every killed, wounded or sick member was immediately replaced with a new one, thus maintaining a constant number) carried spears which terminated in a golden or silver pomegranate at their lower end instead of a spike.[11] This conspicuous display of wealth seems rather impractical for the battlefield. The multi-seeded and Eastern-originating pomegranate is being exploited to symbolize the immense and multi-ethnic Persian Empire. Herodotus has Darius the Great use a pomegranate to praise his most loyal subjects. As the Persian king sits eating a pomegranate, he is questioned as to what he wishes to have as many of as the number of seeds in the fruit. Darius replies 'Men like Megabazus,' complimenting his trusted military commander.[12] Similarly Plutarch tells us that the Persian king Artaxerxes praised a man who gave him a single pomegranate, saying: 'By Mithra, this man wo[uld] speedily make a city great instead of small were he entruste[d] with it.'[13] The idea here is that the small pomegranate is used to represent the large one, its inner quantity of seeds making it far exceed its size.

The pomegranate was valued in Greek medicinal thought. The father of medicine, Hippocrates, recommended the fruit for a number of ailments, including the treatment of eye infections and morning sickness and to aid digestive health. In later Roman times, Pliny the Elder also noted the pomegranate's potential, recording many remedies that made use of the plant, from the treatment of scorpion stings to epilepsy.[14] Pliny even noted that pomegranate rind could be burnt to repel gnats or ground down for use in the making of Roman perfume. The pomegranate is said to have arrived in Rome from Carthage, and was thus known to the Romans as *mala punica* (the Punic apple). In Roman art the pomegranate is most commonly found among the fruits of the wreaths signifying plenty that can be found on the sides of tombs and altars, including the famed Ara Pacis of Augustus. The pomegranate may also be found as a design on ceramic oil lamps of the Roman Empire, as a motif type from Cyprus demonstrates, and another even further east in Israel.

Even into late antiquity, the strong association between the pomegranate and female divinity was not forgotten. A sixth-century AD Byzantine tapestry from Egypt made of wool and linen depicts a very pagan theme, although by this time Christianity had become more predominant. It is a late representation of Hestia, the Greek goddess of the hearth. The goddess of the Hestia Tapestry wears a pomegranate headdress and earrings, emphasizing her role as the Polyolbos ('rich in blessings'). The fruit, with its many seeds, is appropriately evoked in this image of abundance. The blessings

Cypriot pomegranate lamp, 1st century AD.

that Hestia gives out are in the form of pomegranates, each standing for a virtue such as wealth, prosperity or excellence. A Byzantine arch of the Monastery of Apa Apollo in Egypt, from roughly the same date, likewise features the pomegranate as the epitome of plenty, growing upon the running vines that form the arch. The theme is classical, although unlike

The Byzantine Hestia Tapestry, made in Egypt in the 6th century.

the tapestry, the context is purely Christian. The pomegranate would come to play an important role at the Byzantine court during this late antique period. Part of an empress's marriage and coronation involved a ceremonial procession in which she was accompanied by dignitaries who carried three jewel-encrusted marble pomegranates.[15]

The pomegranate still has very strong symbolic value in modern Greece, demonstrating just how enduring ancient ideas and traditions can be. The fruit thus continues to be a favourite decorative motif on houses around the Mediterranean, as well as on textiles and ceramics. The historian Efthymios G. Lazongas notes that in a local tradition from the Greek town of Epidaurus, 'peasants break open a pomegranate on the ploughshare of the plough and mingle the seeds of the pomegranate with the grains to be sown in order to achieve the

desired prosperity."[16] The pomegranate still has funerary connotations in Greece today, as part of a *koliva* offering prepared
in commemoration of the dead. This is a sweet boiled wheat
dish that contains pomegranate arils. Following a Greek
wedding, a pomegranate is traditionally blessed and then
broken on the threshold of the couple's home in the hope of
a long and fruitful marriage. This also may occur at other times
of transition, such as the purchase of a new house or at the
beginning of a New Year.

3
Jewish and Islamic Pomegranates

On its lower hem you shall make pomegranates of blue, purple
and crimson yarns, all around the lower hem, with bells of gold
between them all around – a golden bell and a pomegranate
alternating all around the lower hem of the robe.

Exodus 28:33–4

Pomegranates in Ancient and Modern Judaism

The above quotation is part of a descriptive passage from
Exodus that records how the God of the Israelites com-
manded the way in which high priests' garments were to be
made. The pomegranate figures prominently in this design.
But why would a fruit with such deep roots in pagan fertility cults decorate the garments of priests who worshipped
a male monotheistic deity? Their appearance is probably a
reference to sacrifice: the pomegranate is an elegant way of
representing the blood of the offering, while the bells (also
the shape of the pomegranate flower) recall the sounds that
would accompany the religious experience. After all, the
pomegranate plant already had an important role to play in

sacrifice: a branch of pomegranate wood was traditionally used to make the skewer on which a paschal offering was roasted.[1] The pomegranate garment is also likely to be a patriotic display of Jewish heritage, for in Deuteronomy 8:8 we are told that the pomegranate is one of the plant species identified with the Land of Israel. The fruit was brought to Moses by scouts in a demonstration of the fertility of the Promised Land, and it was under a pomegranate tree that the first king of Israel, Saul, sought shade from the harsh sun (1 Samuel 14:2). The fruit became inextricably linked with Jewish identity and experience, the Midrash reflecting: 'Thus were Israel in Egypt as a heap of stones . . . once they went out they became like a grove of pomegranates. All through the ages when mankind looked upon Israel they were praised.'[2] The Hebrew Bible cites many localities in the Holy Land that came to be named after the fruit, such as Ain-Rimmon (Spring of the Pomegranate) and Sela Rimmon (Rock of the Pomegranate). The death of a pomegranate tree in ancient Jewish culture was considered to be a negative omen, indicating that God was unhappy.[3] Today the pomegranate features as a ubiquitous motif on many items of Judaic art, from jewellery and utensils to protective, prayer-filled mezuzahs affixed to household doorways.

Jewish tradition teaches that the pomegranate is a symbol of righteousness, knowledge and wisdom because it is said to have 613 seeds, each representing one of the 613 *mitzvot* (commandments) of the Torah. Torah scrolls are traditionally decorated with *rimmonim*,[4] a pair of pomegranate-shaped finials, usually made of silver, that are placed over the wooden scroll handles when the text is not in use. It is common practice among Jews to eat pomegranates on Rosh Hashanah, Jewish New Year, in reference to the fruit's erudite nature, but also as a guarantor of the productivity of

Although *rimmonim* Torah covers are found in a variety of shapes today, this example by Itzhak Luvation retains a traditional pomegranate form.

the New Year. On this occasion a prayer is recited over the fruit: 'May it be Your will O Lord our God and the God of Our Fathers, that our good deeds will increase like the seeds of the pomegranate.'

The pomegranate is also included among the fruits presented for Tu Bishvat, a festival that celebrates trees and environmentalism. There is a saying in the Talmud that

'Even thy empty-headed ones are full of good deeds as a pomegranate is of seeds.'[5] The Talmud also gives advice for the dream interpretation of pomegranates: 'Both Abiya and Raba dreamt about a ripening pomegranate. Abiya solved the dream – Thy transactions shall flourish like a pomegranate (meaning they shall be as many as the seeds of one).'[6]

The Jewish physician Rabbi Shabtai Donolo noted the importance of the pomegranate in medicine, suggesting a gargle of pomegranate juice mixed with wine as a remedy for laryngitis. He advised that earache could be treated by grinding up dried pomegranate rinds, mixing with water and pouring this solution into the affected ear.

The pomegranate appears on ancient coins of Judea. It is one of only a few images that appear as a holy symbol on currency, the 'crowned' fruit taking the place of a crowned ruler's head. King Solomon is in fact alleged to have designed his crown based on the crown-like calyx of the pomegranate.

Detail of mosaic in the 6th-century Maon Synagogue.

The modern state of Israel still uses this pomegranate motif on coins and stamps.

One pomegranate in particular, made of hippopotamus ivory that originates from the age of biblical Israel, has caused a stir in modern times. The 44-millimetre-tall pomegranate bears an inscription in Hebrew circling around the neck of the fruit: 'holy to the priests, belonging to the House of Yahweh'. For this reason, it has been speculated that it originated from the sceptre of a high priest who resided at Solomon's Temple, which was said to use the fruit motif heavily in its decorative programme: biblical accounts tell us that two hundred representations of the pomegranates were depicted on each of the two bronze pillars, known as Boaz and Jachin, that marked the entrance to the holy space. The unprovenanced ivory pomegranate itself is generally accepted as an authentic thirteenth-century BC artefact. Uninscribed ivory pomegranates of the same style have been found at the Israeli site of Lachish and in Cypriot tombs. It is the inscription that fuels ongoing debate, since it is considered to be a modern forgery applied to a genuine artefact. The historian Mary Abram sums it up best when she comments: 'While a validated inscription might confirm its use in a temple setting, the fact that alleged forgers used the already-ancient ivory pomegranate to simulate a temple artefact supports its recognition (even by criminals) as a sacred symbol ... no fruit but the pomegranate best combines the diversities of sensory pleasure, earth's seasonal cycles, worldly kingship, and holiness.'[7] It is for this reason that the pomegranate is archaeologically represented in the Jewish art programmes of many ancient synagogues, notably in reliefs and mosaics at Capernaum, Hamat Tiberias, Beth Alpha and Maon.

Some scholarly traditions have identified the pomegranate as the forbidden fruit of the Garden of Eden. It is the pomegranate that best represents decadent and sensuous beauty in passages from the Song of Songs, the narrator at one point flattering his beloved with the simile 'Your cheeks are like halves of a pomegranate behind your veil.' Another story in the Talmud also equates the pomegranate with temptation.[8] This tale concerns Rabbi Hiyya ben-Abba who, being a pious man, prays daily for respite from temptation. His wife overhears him and wonders why he prays so, given that he has abstained from being with her sexually for many years. She thus decides to test him. The wife decks the disguise of a prostitute, walking to and fro in front of the rabbi in order to arouse his attention. She remarks that if the rabbi desires to be with her, her price is a pomegranate retrieved from the highest branch of a certain tree. The rabbi immediately climbs the tree, picks the pomegranate and brings it back to her. Only now, the wife reveals her true identity. Filled with shame at being led into temptation, the rabbi fasts for the rest of his life, until death. The pomegranate functions in the tale as the symbol of his transgression, marking his movement from the spiritual towards more bodily concerns.

Pomegranates for Muslims

Islamic tradition shares with Judaism a great reverence for the pomegranate. Those who eat a pomegranate are considered to have their hearts cleansed and filled with *nūr* (light), rendering them free from sin and able to repel Satan's temptations for forty days. As representations of God, Muhammad and other religious personages are forbidden, stylized images from nature are common in religious art and architecture, and the pomegranate is a popular emblem. As well as being a favourite in manuscript border ornamentation, the pomegranate is a common iconographic trait of Islamic pottery. The styles

Mould-made ceramic bowl from Susa, Iran, 7th–8th century.

of pomegranates on different types of Islamic pottery are demonstrated by three very different examples of vessels, all of which share the pomegranate motif. A common Islamic vessel type is a bronze ewer, characterized by its globular belly, tubular neck and slender beaded handle topped with a thumb-piece cast in the form of a pomegranate. The pomegranate also features on many painted Islamic blue-on-white glazed ceramics, both vessels and tiles. A third type is a unique mould-made vessel adorned with relief decoration featuring images of growing pomegranate trees beneath an upper register bearing a line of Qur'anic poetry. The pomegranate likewise enjoys popularity in Middle Eastern textiles, commonly appearing on both garments and carpets. The reason for the respect given to the fruit may be the result of a Hadith which claims that the Prophet Muhammad told his companions that each pomegranate contains an aril from heaven itself: 'There is not a pomegranate which does not have a pip from one of the pomegranates of the Garden (Jannah) in it.'[9] The consumption

Bronze ewer from Iran, 11th century.

Blue and white ceramic bowl with a central motif of a pomegranate, Iran, *c* 1500.

of arils for the pre-dawn meal of *suhoor* during Ramadan is thus considered to be an appropriate prelude to fasting.

Like Judaism, Islamic tradition attributes to the pomegranate a dangerous, seductive side. The transgressive effect of the fruit is found in a fable about the eighth-century AD caliph Yazid II. Being particularly fond of his singing slave girl Hababa, Yazid shuts himself away with her and orders that he not be disturbed. Together they spend the day eating until Hababa chokes to death on a pomegranate seed that had been playfully thrown into her mouth by the caliph. Abd al-Majid ibn Abdun's retelling of the tale speaks of the seed as being 'preordained'. Yazid is heartbroken and dies a few days later.

Islamic carpet from the Silk Road settlement of Kashgar,
18th–19th century.

The seductive nature of the fruit makes it a suitable means for the downfall of the caliph, who has rejected duty in favour of the company of a low woman. Although the Prophet Mohammad advised pregnant women to eat pomegranates if they wanted beautiful children, an anecdote concerning Allāmah Majlisi, the compiler of a Hadith collection, notes that the fruit needs to be from an appropriate source. When he was a child, Allāmah Majlisi was taken to a mosque with his father. While his father was inside praying, the young boy remained in the courtyard. On finishing his prayer, the father discovered that his son had poked a needle into a water skin that belonged to the mosque, and all the water had spilled out. On hearing of her son's behaviour, Allāmah Majlisi's mother related to her upset husband how this incident had came about. Years before, while she was pregnant with him, she had gone to a neighbour's house and seen a pomegranate tree. She made a prick in one of the pomegranates and sucked out the juice. It was this act that led to the later occurrence at the mosque. The pomegranate has the potential to be a powerful omen both in Islamic and Jewish tradition.

4
Medieval Pomegranates

Go to, sir; you were beaten in Italy for picking a kernel out
of a pomegranate: you are a vagabond and no true traveller
Lafeu in William Shakespeare's
All's Well that Ends Well, Act II Scene 3

The spread of the pomegranate benefited greatly from the
Crusades, as fruit was brought back to various European
nations by many returning knights. New dishes had to be
devised in order to include the fruit in their respective cui-
sines. The *Modus viaticorum preparandorum et salsarum*, an Occitan
cookbook of the fourteenth century AD, includes among its
recipes a dish known as *raymonia*. This recipe must have been
considerably popular, as it even appears in the Middle English
aristocratic cookbook *The Forme of Cury*. The instructions are
as follows:

> If you want to make a raymonia, take hens and cook
> them with salted meat. And take unblanched almonds,
> and wash them in lukewarm water, and grind them very
> strongly, and dilute with hen's broth, and strain. After-
> wards, take pomegranate verjuice or pomegranate wine
> and add it. Then boil it and add enough sugar.[1]

The central roundel from the Hinton St Mary mosaic showing Jesus Christ flanked by pomegranates, early 4th century AD.

This dish is a revision of the Arabic *rummaniya*, a chicken bruet with pomegranate juice, ground almonds and sugar. However, it was much more than recipes that were adopted and adapted in the medieval period, as ancient notions were used to create new and powerful symbols surrounding the pomegranate.

As the medieval Christian world drew on many pagan traits adopted from their classical predecessors, the pomegranate retained the same ideology, borrowed from the Persephone myth. The fruit became associated with the Resurrection of Christ and the eventual resurrection of his believers, instead of the annual resurrection of crops. The central bust of Jesus in the Hinton St Mary mosaic, discovered in the county of

Sandro Botticelli, *Madonna of the Pomegranate*, 1487, tempera on wood.

Dorset, England, uses two pomegranates in conjunction with the Chi-Rho symbol to form a somewhat unconventional halo. It is from a Roman villa of the fourth century AD and is the earliest-known image of Christ in Britain and the only known portrait of Christ used in a mosaic pavement. To an audience of recently converted Roman pagans, the image of pomegranates would immediately conjure images of rebirth. The many seeds of the pomegranate protected inside a single rind came to stand for the Church itself, which unified people in faith. The pomegranate and its symbolism would survive in later icons and religious paintings. In the common scene of Mary holding the infant Jesus, one of the pair is sometimes represented holding a split pomegranate, or both have pomegranate

Three pomegranates top this 14th-century ivory triptych of the Passion of Christ. From the central split pomegranate pour arils that form a decorative border of the entire ivory.

South Netherlandish Unicorn Tapestry, 15th century. The beast is chained to a pomegranate tree with wounds that drip pomegranate arils in place of blood. The meaning of the letters AE hanging from the tree branches are unknown, although it is speculated that these may be monogram initials of a pair of newlyweds.

seeds fall upon them. The most famous example of this type is by the Italian Renaissance master Sandro Botticelli. The open pomegranate, with its seeds bursting forth, is likened to Christ bursting forth from the tomb. The same themes are evoked in a fourteenth-century ivory. Pomegranates sprout from the central panel of a triptych in which the Crucifixion is depicted, forecasting the Resurrection.

The *Geoponica* is a tenth-century Byzantine encyclopaedia of land cultivation, which includes mention of a practice involving pomegranates during this period. The text states that ancient Africans believed that a pomegranate branch was so powerful that any wild beast would become terrified in its presence. The author of the *Geoponica* thus advises that a pomegranate branch should be laid at the entrance of the home for the protection of the household. This notion is based on an earlier Roman belief, for Pliny in his *Natural History* claims that a pomegranate branch will repel snakes.[2]

One mythical beast that the pomegranate had an effect on was the unicorn, popularized in medieval art as a mythical symbol of Christ. Known for its purity, the unicorn could only be captured by a virgin, after which it could be tamed by being tied to a pomegranate tree. A Netherlandish tapestry from the fifteenth century shows a wounded unicorn bleeding pomegranate seeds while chained to a pomegranate tree, further emphasizing the fertility potential already signified by the beast's prominent horn. Being symbolic of marriage, the image of the unicorn tied to the pomegranate tree, with the red seeds of the fruit spilling on him, functions as an allegory for the bridal sheets.

The twelfth-century historian William of Malmesbury took great interest in recording the ways in which people of the Middle Ages died. No anecdote he tells is stranger than one which includes a delightful image of a pomegranate. William relates that it is 'well known' that if any man were bitten by a leopard in Asia, a group of mice would subsequently plan an attack on his boat, with the objective of urinating on his wounds. This, according to William, would cause the man to die. The thousands of mice would row to meet their victim 'in the rinds of pomegranates, the insides of which they had eaten'.[3] This is not the only instance of the pomegranate rind being associated with seafaring. Much more recently, in the nineteenth century, the archaeologist Sir Austen Henry Layard, while exploring ancient sites in Western Asia, observed that raft men on the Tigris preserved the suppleness of the skins used to build their boats by rubbing them with pomegranate rinds.[4] William's tale probably refers to this technique of using the rind for buoyancy, a practice which most likely had much older origins.

Pomegranates featured in medieval architecture, the fruit-fulness of the seeds making it a fitting symbol for evoking the Virgin Mary in church designs. The architectural example of the Pilastri Acritani demonstrates this. Its two pillars are carved with symmetrical and stylized pomegranate plants, each topped with a single fruit growing from vases. Now standing in Venice, they were traditionally regarded as trophies of the Venetian victory over the Genoese at Acre, Israel, in the thirteenth century. This however was proved false in 1960, with the discovery of the sixth-century church of St Polyeuctus in Istanbul, which bore identical stylistic traits. So how did they get to Venice? The pillars were probably part of the booty taken back after the sack of Constantinople by the Venetian-led Fourth Crusade in 1204. The church of St Polyeuctus, from which the pillars originate, dates from the reign of Justin 1 and was commissioned by the noblewoman Anicia Juliana. The choice of using pomegranates heavily in its architectural design is probably in tribute to her femininity. The imagery

The Pilastri Acritani in front of the Basilica di San Marco, originally part of the Church of St Polyeuctus in Constantinople.

on the Pilastri Acritani is probably also an evocation of the Solomonic Temple, which, as discussed in Chapter Three, featured pomegranates prominently in its design.

The pomegranate was used to convey a message by many well-known figures of the Middle Ages. After conquering Granada in 1492 (and subsequently adding a pomegranate to

Imperial crest giving the pomegranate a prominent position in the centre of the Cross of Burgundy and the Hapsburg firesteels, on the 16th-century Palace of Charles v at the Alhambra of Granada, Spain.

her coat of arms), Isabella I is reported to have stood with a pomegranate in her hand and declared, 'Just like the pomegranate, I will take over Andalusia seed by seed.'[5] Granada is of course the Moorish city in Spain, named after the Spanish word for our favourite fruit. From medieval times until today the pomegranate has featured prominently in the architecture of the city. Tourists exploring the city today will soon become aware of modern representations of the pomegranate on street signs, drains, church pews, fountains, bollards and fence spikes and as a logo of many shops. One of the gateways to the city's famed Alhambra is topped with the allegorical figures of Peace and Abundance alongside three split pomegranates. The coat of arms of the city likewise features the fruit.

The pomegranate became an emblem on the coat of arms of Isabella's daughter Catherine of Aragon (1485–1536), the first wife of Henry VIII. Through the queen, the fruit was introduced into England at this time, and is often conjoined with the Tudor rose in iconography.[6] The pomegranate featured prominently during the festivities held in honour of Catherine and Henry's marriage, such as in displays of gilded fruits. A field was planted with roses and pomegranates next to one another to denote the union of England and Spain.[7] However, the pomegranate proved to be of no assistance to her fertility, and when Henry and Catherine were unable to produce a surviving male heir, the king eventually divorced her in favour of a new marriage to Anne Boleyn. Still today people honour Catherine, placing flowers and pomegranates on her grave in Peterborough Cathedral.

When Anne Boleyn became queen, she adopted a new coat of arms showing a white falcon surrounded by Tudor roses. Anne's falcon is sometimes depicted hacking up Catherine's pomegranate (as in an illumination from page four of *Motets et Chansons*, a music book owned by Anne). This image inspired

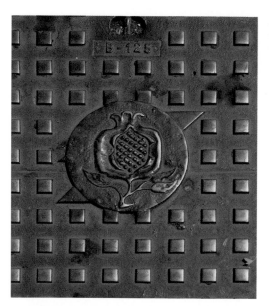

Manhole cover of a sewer in Granada, Spain.

Street sign in Granada, Spain.

Pomegranate
bollard in
Granada, Spain.

Pomegranate
fountain in
Granada, Spain.

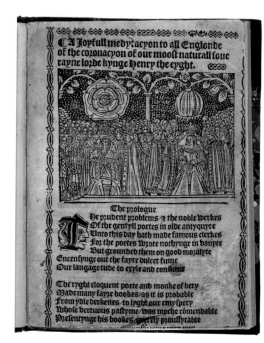

Woodcut depicting a celebration of the joint coronation of Henry VIII and Catherine of Aragon, from a 16th-century manuscript. Henry sits beneath the Tudor Rose of England, while Catherine is under the pomegranate.

the creation of a piece of silk embroidery by the artist Suky Best that she attributes to Anne Boleyn's mother, Elizabeth, which depicts Anne's falcon pecking at the pomegranate. Capturing the spirit of her sentiment towards Catherine, the French text around it contains Anne's personal motto: *Ainsi sera, groinge qui groinge* ('That's the way it's going to be, however much people grumble').

In terms of textiles of the period, the pomegranate was a favoured motif embroidered on clothes during the medieval era and until the seventeenth century. It was adapted from the Islamic East, elaborate pomegranate patterns now status symbols adorning garments worn by elites of European society. Paintings show the fruit worn by both women (as in portraits of Mary Clopton and Eleonora di Toledo) and men (as worn by one of the Eastern kings in Gentile da Fabriano's *Adoration of the Magi*). The sixteenth-century Henry IV of France (who was known for passing the Edict of Nantes, which allowed for religious freedom, thus ending civil war between Catholics and Protestants) wore the pomegranate as a heraldic badge. He chose as his motto 'Sour, yet sweet,' comparing the nature of

Elizabeth Boleyns Embroidery, c. 1530 (A Fictional Embroidery That May or May Not Have Existed). Sewn, damaged and restored by the artist Suky Best in 2003, and presented as though it were a real artefact.

Robert Peake the Elder, portrait of a woman traditionally identified as Mary Clopton wearing a pomegranate-textile dress, 16th century.

the pomegranate with his belief that a king should be firm but fair with his subjects. The Holy Roman Emperor Maximilian I of Austria likewise used the pomegranate as his emblem, and it is held by the monarch in a notable portrait of 1519 by Albrecht Dürer. In Maximilian's portrait, the pomegranate

Holy Roman Emperor Maximilian I holds a pomegranate as his globus cruciger in this portrait by Albrecht Dürer, 1519.

arils symbolize the ruler's subjects: diverse but held together under the rule of his empire.

Medieval medical thought held the pomegranate in high esteem. The fruit is the attribute of the fifteenth-century saint and medical doctor San Juan de Dios (St John of God), who devoted his life to the service of the poor and sick from his hospital in Granada. Statues of the saint depict him holding a

The symbol of San Juan de Dios held by a statue in Granada, Spain.

pomegranate with a cross coming out of its calyx. The sixteenth century saw the Royal College of Physicians of London adopt the pomegranate into their coat of arms. The restorative fruit rests beneath an outstretched arm, gripped by a hand descending from the heavens. It is still their logo today. In medieval humour theory, the pomegranate was considered warm and moist in nature, the same traits attributed to the human male.

Pomegranates were thus prescribed by medieval physicians to counterbalance phlegm and coughs, which were cold and dry in nature. When eaten before a meal, pomegranates supposedly stimulated the appetite, and were considered to have aphrodisiac properties. In medieval thought, the womb of a woman was a beast with a mind of its own, with the ability to wander around a woman's body causing ailments; for example, when it moved up into the head, it would cause headaches. The *Trotula*, a medieval medical text, specifies that a wandering womb that had descended from the body could be restored by bathing in water that had been blended with various berries, nuts and seeds, including pomegranate arils and rinds.[8] Throughout the *Trotula*, the pomegranate is linked with conditions unique to the female experience, another passage recommending rubbing pomegranate on the feet to reduce the foot swelling that occurs during pregnancy. The text even notes the fruit's use in cosmetic treatments, claiming that a mixture of ground pomegranate, water, vinegar, oak apple and alum could be used to dye one's hair black.

5

Pomegranate Production and Culture Today

The pomegranate is one of the sexiest foods on earth.
Its crimson shade is the colour of desire. They're messy and
sticky, and because there's no other way to eat a pomegranate
than with your fingers, the act of consuming the juicy little
seeds becomes a sensuous act of play.

Amy Reiley, named Master of Gastronomy by Le Cordon Bleu

Today's centres of the pomegranate industry are Iran, Afghanistan, Turkey, India, Israel, Spain and the United States, with its Californian plantations becoming increasingly significant on the world stage. Spain remains the only major producer of pomegranates for commercial export in the European Union. India exports heavily to the United Arab Emirates, Oman and the UK. The fruit holds a symbolic significance in the local economies of many Middle Eastern and Central Asian countries, as well as the Mediterranean. As of 2014 Iran and India remain the world's largest producers of the fruit. For many countries today it is the symbolic rather than the economic value of the pomegranate that has resulted in it becoming such a source of national pride. This is epitomized in Mexico, where the traditional dish *chiles en nagoda* recreates the colours of the national flag. The green is rendered with chilli, the white with nut sauce and the red with pomegranate arils.

America and the Western Pomegranate Industry

The pomegranate arrived in the New World via Spanish missionaries. When Hernán Cortés conquered the Aztecs in the sixteenth century, pomegranate trees, the symbol of Spain, were planted in Mexico as a marker of the conquest. Spanish settlers later introduced the fruit to Texas, California and Arizona in the eighteenth century. Peter Collinson wrote of his high esteem for the fruit to his Philadelphian botanist friend John Bartram in 1762:

> Don't use the Pomegranate inhospitably, a stranger that has come so far to pay his respects to thee. Don't turn him adrift in the wide world; but plant it against the side of thy house, nail it close to the wall. In this manner it thrives wonderfully with us, and flowers beautifully, and bears fruit . . . of all trees this is most salutiferous to mankind.[1]

By 1771 even Thomas Jefferson had planted pomegranates at Monticello, his plantation in Virginia. Pomegranate-shaped beads are found on the distinctive Native American 'squash blossom' necklace design associated with the Navajo tribe. These were first made in the nineteenth century by Navajo silversmiths who learnt this art from the Spanish. The turquoise and silver beads in the necklace (round with a calyx), which have been misidentified as squash blossoms, were in fact adapted from the trouser and shirt buttons worn by the

Spanish, which were in the form of their national motif, the Granadian pomegranate.

Today the best known cultivar of pomegranate, the 'Wonderful' variety, originates from California, where it was first propagated in 1896 from a cutting brought west from Florida. The 'Wonderful' is known for its juiciness and sweetness. It is fairly resistant to rind cracking, the blight of the pomegranate industry. Especially after it rains, ripe pomegranates have a habit of cracking open and turning almost inside out. In nature, this splitting of the fruit is a biological device allowing for seeds to distribute themselves.

Despite the pomegranate's appearance early in America's history, the fruit remained an oddity in the u.s. until recently, an exotic food item enjoyed mainly by immigrants and Americans who discovered it abroad. The debut of the Pom Wonderful juice company in 2002 (with their successful, if not sometimes misleading, advertising campaign promoting the fruit), and the publication of research that showed the high antioxidant, dietary fibre and vitamin value of pomegranate, as well as its potential anti-carcinogenic properties, have resulted in the fruit becoming available to a much wider Western audience. Studies done recently even showed that microbicides obtained from pomegranate juice are effective against HIV, preventing the entrance of the virus into the body. The fruit has the capability to absorb radiation and has been used in cancer research. The pomegranate received the hallowed 'superfood' status in an article published in *Men's Health* in 2008, and suddenly demand for it escalated. It is now commonly found in sauces, soft drinks (sodas), ice creams, cakes, teas, chewing gum, jellies, chocolates, salad dressings, liqueurs and the famous syrup grenadine, produced from the fruit for use in drinks.[2] Many brands have experimented with the release of limited-edition pomegranate-flavoured varieties of their product: pomegranate-flavoured liquorice produced by Darrell Lea confectioners, Häagen-Dazs's pomegranate ice cream, pomegranate-flavoured 7UP. Pomegranate-flavoured snack products have occasionally come under criticism, as the companies that create them tend to stress the high antioxidant and nutritional value of the pomegranate in their marketing campaigns despite fizzy drinks and sweets not being health foods.

The cosmetic industry has also begun to produce an increasing number of pomegranate-based soaps and body creams, the fruit being known for its sun-protection, anti-ageing, hydration and anti-inflammatory properties. A company devoted entirely to pomegranate skincare products, Pomega5, was established in California in 2005. The fruit retains its ancient connotations of sensuality in the modern market, pomegranate-flavoured personal lubricant being available from several companies (with charming brand names like 'Wet' and 'Sliquid'). Notable designers Jo Malone and Marc Jacobs have even produced pomegranate-scented lines of their fragrances. The desire for pomegranate flavouring has thus resulted in a large and growing market, which often cannot meet demand, for juice concentrate. Sixteen thousand acres of pomegranate plantation currently exist in California, but with the American pomegranate industry steadily on the rise, acreage is anticipated to increase considerably in coming years. The annual fresh harvest for the area currently yields about u.s.$60 million worth of fruit. Today the u.s. leads the world in increasing consumption of the fruit per capita: in 2002 Americans consumed ten times as many pomegranates annually as they did two years earlier in 2000. The USDA Agricultural Research Service at Davis, California, has a programme of distributing free cuttings of an assortment of cultivars to members of the general public interested in trying to grow their own pomegranate plant.[3] They hold tasting events in which different pomegranate varieties are ranked on their flavour.

The Afghani Pomegranate Industry

Another country with a developing pomegranate industry, this time in the East, is Afghanistan. Recent war and political turmoil in the country have greatly disrupted this industry and had a serious impact on exportation of the fruit to an international audience. However, 2008 saw the beginnings of a re-emergence of the pomegranate industry in Afghanistan. In 2008 Afghanistan hosted its first international pomegranate fair in the hope that its farmers would become more renowned for producing the fruit than for opium poppy production. The fair has since become an annual event. Loren Stoddard of the American agency for international development u.s. Aid, which sponsored the fair, said that 'We want one product that could be the symbol of the new Afghanistan that will lead onto other products.' As part of the 2008 fair a tribal meeting covering the entire Nangarhar Province was called, with two hundred elders who agreed to finish poppy cultivation and switch to growing pomegranates. The tribal elders conducted a symbolic ceremony in a farmer's field, which they cleared of opium poppies, planting the first pomegranate tree saplings in their place. The year 2008 also saw increasing international demand, which resulted in the local market prices rising from 55 u.s. cents a kilogram to $1.60 a kilogram within a twelve-month period. The 2010 Afghan-Pak Trade and Transit Agreement has assisted the exportation of the pomegranate to its major buyers, permitting Afghan traders to export local agriculture produce to Indian and Pakistani markets via the Wagah border post. Of his country's fruit, the Afghani agricultural minister

Mohammed Asif Rahini believes, 'there are other countries producing pomegranates but no other country can compete with ours and it's God's blessing that we have this quality.'[4] The country now exports up to 80,000 tons of the fruit a year. The extent to which the pomegranate has come to symbolize this region of the world today has resulted in the fruit lending its name to the Middle Eastern affairs blog of the magazine *The Economist*.

Production Methods

Pomegranate plants generally will not grow fruit for the first three to five years, and for this to occur pruning is necessary, as fruit are produced at the tips of new growth. Pomegranate trees are capable of self-pollination, since they have a hermaphroditic flower. However, only 45 per cent of flowers on pomegranate trees that pollinate themselves will produce fruit. There is a great advantage in cross-pollinating with a second plant, as this increases fruit yield to 68 per cent.[5] Wind is not an effective carrier of pollen, as it can be with other plants, and thus one must rely on either insects (mainly bees) to spread pollen or hand-pollination. This is usually achieved by applying a brush or swab to each yellowish, pollen-covered anther of the flower. The brush is then used to transfer the pollen grains to the sticky, receptive stigma on a flower of the desired pomegranate plant. Pollinated flowers lose their petals and mature into clusters of fruit that ripen within seven months. Productive plants can yield as many as 10 tons of fruit per plantation acre.

The pomegranate generally loves heat and is at optimum production in an arid climate. Pomegranate trees are reasonably hardy, and are fairly frost-, flood-, saline- and drought-tolerant. However the fruit can still suffer as a result of these factors, which may affect the taste, increase fall-off or stunt the growth of plants. The pomegranate plant has a xylopode, an underground stem that stocks nutrients, which is able to restore the bush if it dies back after harsh environmental conditions. Some cultivars are more adaptable to environmental conditions than others, such as the 'Agat' variety, which is capable of thriving in the snow of Russia. The people of Uzbekistan, to prevent their pomegranates from dying during their harsh winters, pile dirt over the bushes until they are completely buried and then wait until the following spring to unearth them.[6] Other methods used in Europe to prevent pomegranates freezing include growing them in a polytunnel to keep the plants at a constant temperature. The pomegranate will grow in a variety of soil types, be they black, sandy, lime-rich or dry and rocky. It is best cultivated in alkaline soils, although those with heavy clay content may lighten fruit colour. Several insects pester plant growth, including *Virachola isocrates*, which has come to be known as the pomegranate butterfly. It lays egg larvae on the plant, which when hatched burrow into the fruit.

Once the pomegranate is cut (not picked, as this will damage the plant) from the tree, it will cease ripening. Each fruit, which is in fact classed as a berry (defined as a fleshy fruit that encases seeds, produced from a single ovary), can contain 200 to 1,400 seeds. Often the fruit is grown for the express purpose of drinking rather than eating the arils. The traditional method of juicing in Iran resembles making wine: the cut-open fruits are stamped on in a clay tub by a person wearing special shoes. Popular Western methods for juicing the fruit include the use of a basket press or hydraulic extraction. The juice is usually filtered before consumption, due to the high tannin content of the fruit. The fruit is sometimes fermented to make pomegranate wine.

Dr Gregory Levin

If one man truly deserves a place in the history of the pomegranate, it is the Soviet scientist Dr Gregory Levin. Levin, who is somewhat of a hero in pomegranate circles, devoted his life to the study of the fruit from the agricultural research station of Garrigala in Turkmenistan. For the forty years he was at Garrigala, from 1961 to 2001, he achieved the world's largest pomegranate germplasm collection of 1,117 varieties. Levin went on hikes around Central Asia and the Caucasus in search of wild pomegranate varieties. Pomegranate varieties were also sent to Levin from contacts abroad, including Egypt, Algeria and the Himalayas. Levin bred the wild pomegranates in order to create new cultivars, using selection and mutation to develop desirable qualities. Frost-resistance, sweet flavour, high juice content, softness of seed and rind-cracking were particular concerns. Studies included the preservation and growth of pomegranate seeds stored in liquid nitrogen. He sent seedlings of the varieties he developed to a number of countries, including the u.s., where they are still grown today.

However, his story became one of a paradise lost. The Eden that was Garrigala started its demise with the breakdown of the Soviet Union:

> When Turkmenistan became an independent country in 1991, new governmental agencies began supervising us, replacing the ussr. They changed the name of the station. The new government of Turkmenistan apparently did not need science, and in particular, punicology – the study of pomegranates. They gradually stopped financing the station.[7]

The pomegranates at Garrigala began dying from drought. For lack of a pump, workers carried water in cans from a nearby river, and even used sewage water to irrigate the fruit. In 2001 Levin was forced to immigrate to Israel. He discovered a few years later that his pomegranate plantations had been destroyed to make way for vegetables, on order of the Turkmenistan Ministry of Agriculture. Some of Levin's pomegranate cultivars were grown in his new home of Israel, where the water-saving technique of covering the plants in nets to reduce evaporation was utilized. But visiting the Israeli plantation in 2003 was not a positive experience for him. The pomegranate varieties that he developed, which were producing fruit with positive qualities, had been re-identified with numbers rather than the names he had given them. This limited researchers abroad, particularly in the United States, from having access to propagate the desirable pomegranate cultivars that Levin had written about.[8] Today Levin voices his concern for the depleting numbers of wild pomegranates that are becoming endangered due to human pressures, stating that we must

> preserve the biodiversity of the pomegranate. Cultivated varieties of pomegranate are artefacts, creations of civilization and evidence of a very long, incredible history, the way a Rafael [sic] or a Brueghel painting or a Bach fugue is an artefact to protect and preserve for the future.[9]

Nurse Pomegranate

In his memoirs, Levin wrote of the pomegranate's use as a health tonic in his homeland. Pomegranate juice was administered to astronauts, miners, submariners and pilots in the USSR to sustain workers. Even the intergalactic research monkeys on Soviet satellites were fed a mixture of pomegranate and rosehips to maintain their health.[10] We have seen that the pomegranate has been valued for its high vitamin content and medicinal traits from ancient times, and the restorative quality of the fruit in myth and legend has considerably influenced the perceptions that surround the pomegranate in medicine (and probably vice versa). Folk medicines hold the pomegranate in reverence as a form of treatment and prevention for a wide range of ailments; it is thought to accelerate wound healing as well as lessen pain and inflammation, and to help with diabetes, headaches, jaundice, cardiovascular disease, nausea, weight management, nosebleeds, asthma, gingivitis, ulcers, haemorrhoids, depression and respiratory infections, to name just a few. Certain properties are specific to particular pomegranate varieties. For example the Kara-Nar, a black fruit, is used to treat dysentery and vitiligo. In traditional Indian Ayurvedic medicine the pomegranate is a recommended food, its sour-sweetness establishing balance in the bodies of people who are ruled by the hot and fiery Pitta dosha type. It is commonly used in Indian cuisine in the form of medicinal Anardana powder, made from dried and ground pomegranate seeds. Ayurveda utilizes the fruit as a treatment for numerous conditions, such as using pomegranate juice eye drops to prevent cataracts. Not all research in the medicinal effects of the pomegranate has been positive, however, as consumption of the fruit is also known to interfere with certain pharmaceutical drugs.

One controversial use in folk medicine that has sparked scientific experimentation and much spilling of ink is that of the pomegranate's application as a contraceptive and abortifacient. Both taken orally and applied directly on the vagina, the pomegranate is said to trigger contractions in the uterus.

Chinese vase with modelled pomegranate around the neck, 18th century.

One scientific study from the 1970s attempted to demonstrate this in animals.[11] Female rats, fed pomegranate, had a 72 per cent decline in fertility rates, while guinea-pig subjects had a 100 per cent reduction. A forty-day withdrawal from pomegranate consumption saw the fertility of both species restored to normal. A 2003 report from Chhattisgarh, India, notes the use of pomegranate for birth control.[12] The seeds of the fruit are ground into a powder and mixed with sesame oil, then placed in the vagina at the end of the menstrual cycle. Such a vaginal suppository has been known as far back as ancient Mesopotamian times, as demonstrated by an Assyrian cuneiform text that refers to the soaking of wool in pomegranate for placement inside a woman.[13] The pharmacological historian John M. Riddle argues that the pomegranate's ancient use in birth control supports the idea that the pomegranate is the fruit of the biblical tree of knowledge.[14] God's displeasure over the eating of the fruit was due to its contraceptive ability. Riddle believes that the pomegranate likewise became a symbol of the Mesopotamian sex goddess Inanna/Ishtar for its ability to control fertility, being utilized by her sacred temple prostitutes (offering sex as a conduit to the divine) so they could avoid pregnancy. The pomegranate's ability to control fertility is attributed to its high concentration of the female sex hormone oestrogen, which today is used in the manufacture of pharmaceutical contraceptive pills. This whole idea suggests that the enduring symbol of the pomegranate, with its abundance of seeds, as the benevolent provider of fertility is a front for the fruit's darker nature as one that reverses fertility. Research in this area is far from conclusive, however: some prenatal specialists advise that pregnant women avoid pomegranate consumption, while others suggest it is beneficial to the developing foetus and may prevent pregnancy complications like eclampsia.

Pomegranate in Asia: Japan and China

The pomegranate arrived in China in the second century BC, via the Silk Road. In ancient Chinese poetry, it is not the fruit but the pomegranate flower that is the image of beauty.

Many poets compare the flower to a skirt, as Wan Ch'u of the eighth century AD does: 'Her eyebrow paint eclipses daylily hues; The red skirt causes pomegranate flowers to die from envy.'[15] The type of pomegranate grown in China is mainly a yellow-skinned variety. Yellow is an important colour in Chinese culture, and is considered the most beautiful, being symbolic of the earth, luck and royalty. Thus the Chinese consider the pomegranate one of the three blessed fruits, the others being the citron and the peach. The numerous seeds within the pomegranate are said to symbolize the good fortune of having many male offspring, as the Chinese word for the pomegranate seed, zi, is also the word for sons. It has become associated with weddings, arils sometimes being scattered on the bedcovers of the bride and groom to guarantee conception. In traditional Chinese medicine, pomegranate is regarded as a yin tonic that cools and hydrates the body. A dessert of Thai origin that enjoys popularity all over Asia is known as mock pomegranate. It is made by boiling pieces of Chinese water chestnut covered in tapioca flour and red food colouring, and serving these in a dish of shaved ice, rose syrup and evaporated milk. The red chestnut pieces look just like arils, giving the dessert its name.

In Japan, the pomegranate, which is known as *zakuro*, does not have much of a role in national cuisine. Although it is enjoyed in the form of *zakuro-shu*, pomegranate seeds soaked in liquor, the main significance of the fruit in Japan falls in the religious sphere. The pomegranate is associated with Kishibojin, a goddess of children and motherhood. In Japanese iconography, Kishibojin is usually shown suckling an infant while holding a pomegranate in her right hand. Pomegranate imagery adorns the temples of this goddess, who is worshipped by women who are trying to have children. People leave wooden house-shaped plaques with pomegranates painted on them,

Kujaku Myoo holds a pomegranate across his chest in this 12th-century hanging scroll.

Ohara Shoson, *Cockatoo and Pomegranate*, 1927.

known as *ema*, at shrines for the goddess. Mythology, however, tells us that Kishibojin was not always benevolent. She was initially a violent Hindu she-demon known as Hariti who lived on the flesh of children. She is said to have been converted and cured of her child-eating habits by the Buddha, who taught her to redirect her bloodlust by eating the crunchy and bloody seeds of the pomegranate. Another divine figure, Kujaku Myoo, likewise holds a pomegranate as his attribute. He protects individuals from both physical and spiritual poisoning, using his pomegranate to repel evil spirits. Pomegranates often feature in Japanese woodblock prints and also as netsuke, miniature ivory or wooden sculptures that act as fasteners for pouches, hung from the waist by a cord. Notable are the Japanese wood-block artist Ohara Shoson's (1877–1945) two prints, both of which feature the motif of a cheeky cockatoo sitting on a branch of a pomegranate tree, some of the fruit of which have split open, exposing their seeds.

Another Buddhist tale uses the pomegranate to teach an important lesson. This story begins by noting that the Buddha constantly carries a small drum with him that he claims will be played on the day a person comes to him with the greatest sacrifice of all. A rich maharaja, keen to earn such a boasting right, comes to the Buddha, offering him a vast treasure. The Buddha does not sound his drum. An old beggar woman then approaches and offers him a single pomegranate. The Buddha takes the fruit and without delay begins playing the little drum. The maharaja is angered by this, to which the Buddha replies:

> It is natural for a Maharaja to offer gold. But what great sacrifice is made when a hungry old women offers the pomegranate fruit to the Guru despite her hunger. She did not care even for her life and gave the fruit. What greater sacrifice can there be? It is not sacrifice to offer what is

superfluous for you. True sacrifice means giving up that which is most dear to you, that which you value most.[16]

The inner plentifulness of the fruit exceeds the outer grandeur of material wealth.

Celebrating the Pomegranate

Various peoples in modern times have honoured the pomegranate in festivals. One such group are the people of Azerbaijan, who hold an annual pomegranate fair in the town of Goychay. The pomegranate festival takes place every October, combining local cuisine featuring the pomegranate with traditional Azerbaijani music and dance. A favourite dish is *nasharab*, a savoury sauce made of pomegranate that is usually served with fish. The festival typically features competitions, such as a prize for the largest pomegranate, a pomegranate costume contest and a timed pomegranate eating/squeezing contest. The extent to which the pomegranate is linked with Azerbaijani identity was demonstrated by its use in the official logo for the 2015 European Games, held in Azerbaijan's capital, Baku. Designed by Adam Yunisov, the logo brings together five elements of the host country's culture: water, fire, a carpet and the legendary Simurg bird are all enclosed within the shape of a pomegranate. Trees covered in pomegranates feature prominently in the decorative programme of the eighteenth-century Azerbaijani Palace of Shaki Khans. In honour of the special place of the pomegranate in the hearts of the Azerbaijani people, a large novelty pomegranate has been built in Goychay. There are many other instances of pomegranate-shaped sculptural monuments around the world. A huge gold bowl stacked with a pyramid of red pomegranates features in Shahrdari Square in

Pomegranate tree illustration inside Azerbaijan's Shaki Khans Palace.

Saveh, Iran. Another example of the fruit used in architecture is a huge mosaic pomegranate by the artist Ruslan Sergeev, which is on public display in Jerusalem. The mosaic medium, using hundreds of tile shards affixed to the outer skin of the fruit, effectively evokes the idea of plenty that is normally associated with the multitudinous internal seeds.

Tehran likewise celebrates its 'ruby from paradise' in festivities. Pomegranate producers from around Iran congregate at a festival allowing for the tasting and exchange of a variety

Celebrations at the 2011 pomegranate festival in Goychay, Azerbaijan.

of cultivars. Works of art featuring the pomegranate are put on display, and dances incorporating the fruit are performed. The 2011 ceremony featured the world's largest pomegranate cake, decorated with representations of the fruit and weighing 800 kg (1,764 lb). An Iranian postal stamp decorated with the fruit was also released for the event. Wish trees feature at the festival, to which are attached pomegranate ornaments. From these hang scrolls containing lines of Hafiz's poetry, which pose a solution to a problem faced by an individual. This classical Persian poet of the fourteenth century once wrote that 'when love mocks, ruby tears fall heavy as pomegranates.' The beloved Persian poet Rumi likewise praised the pomegranate in the thirteenth century, advising that 'If you buy a pomegranate, buy one whose ripeness has caused it to be cleft open with a seed-revealing smile . . . through its wide-open mouth it shows its heart, like a pearl in the jewel box of spirit.'[17]

Mosaic pomegranate by Ruslan Sergeev, Jerusalem.

Pomegranate sculpture in Shahrdari Square, Saveh, Iran.

Another notable festival in celebration of the fruit occurs in the 'Heart of Pomegranate Country', Madera, California. As well as cooking demonstrations, a highlight of the fair is a competition known as the 'Pomegranate Grenade Launch' which involves firing pomegranates at targets from a large slingshot. Skydivers perform an airshow in which they hold pomegranates while parachuting into the event, which is held at the Madera airport in November. In 2013 the event was advertised in a humorous YouTube video featuring the mayor of Madera rapping to a parody cover of Macklemore's 2013 song 'Thrift Shop'.

Pop Culture

There are several references to the pomegranate in popular culture, an appropriate prelude leading us into our next chapter on the fruit in art. This list is continually growing as more people are inspired by the unusual nature of the pomegranate.

Pop singer Katy Perry uses a pomegranate as lipstick in the music video for her song 'Roar'. Adam Lambert's music video for the song 'Better than I Know Myself' features the musician crushing a pomegranate, causing the blood-like juice to spew from his hands. The pomegranate syrup grenadine is paid homage to in Lana del Rey's song 'Bel Air', and the character Michael Scott in the American TV show *The Office* claims straight grenadine as his drink. Anne Baxter as Nefertiri in the 1956 film version of *The Ten Commandments* attempts to seduce Moses, describing her own lips as 'moist and red like a pomegranate' in contrast to his wife's lips, which are 'chafed and dry as the desert sand'. The comedy film *Her Alibi* (1989) features a struggling mystery novelist who writes the lines 'Her breasts squashed against him like ripe pomegranates,' creating a sensual scene using the same kind of phraseology that we have seen in Arabic folklore.

The pomegranate has even impacted the everyday lexicon. The French word for pomegranate, *grenade*, was given to the hand-tossed explosive weapon, evoking the seed-scattering properties of our favourite fruit. The red seeds reflect the destructive blood-spilling caused by weaponry and war. The slang term 'pom' or 'pommy', used by Australians and New Zealanders to describe the British, is a contraction of pomegranate, and refers to the speedy reddening of the skin caused by sun exposure that occurs in people of English origin.[18] The term may alternatively have developed from the use of the word 'pomegranate' as Australian rhyming slang for 'immigrant'.

The pomegranate features in the artwork of two cards from the Rider-Waite tarot deck, first published in 1910 and still the most popular deck available one hundred years later. In the High Priestess card a woman stands in front of a curtain that is covered in pomegranates in reference to the fact that she is seated inside Solomon's Temple, marked by the columns featuring the letters B and J. These are the pillars Boaz and Jachin (here representing light and dark), which, as discussed in Chapter Three, were also noted in the Bible to have been encrusted with pomegranates. The Empress card features a woman reclining amid a field of grain, wearing a robe embroidered in a repeated pomegranate motif. Both these cards use the pomegranate to evoke a scene of fertility. Like the fruit, the presence of a High Priestess in a reading concerns mystery and the divine, while the Empress is associated with sex, motherhood and growth.

The image of plentifulness that the pomegranate evokes is satirized in an amusing hoax advertisement for the all-in-one device the Pomegranate NS08 mobile phone. Launched in 2008, the website www.pomegranatephone.com claims that

Morris & Co., bird and pomegranate wallpaper, 1926.

the ruby-red phone features a variety of inbuilt properties including a video projector, live voice translator, harmonica, coffee maker and razor. The website states that the phone has a battery the size and shape of a pomegranate aril that has the capacity to keep the phone running for five days. While exploring the features advertised, one is soon redirected to an information page about the region of Nova Scotia. The whole website is an elaborate advertisement, not for a new phone, but for tourism in the Canadian province (where 'you can get *everything* you want in one place'). Although the advert features the fruit rolling around and the seeds splattering, Nova Scotia does not in fact have a pomegranate industry of its own. Elsewhere, in real electronics, the pomegranate has inspired researchers at Stanford University's SLAC National Accelerator Laboratory in the development of a new lithium ion battery that holds a cluster of tiny silicon particles in a hard carbon rind, in replication of arils in the fruit.

6

The Pomegranate in Modern Literature, Art and Film

Guarded treasure, honeycomb partitions,
Richness of flavour,
Pentagonal architecture.
The rind splits; seeds fall –
Crimson seeds in azure bowls,
Or drops of gold in dishes of enamelled bronze.

André Gide, *Les Nourritures terrestres*, trans. Dorothy Bussy

The use of the pomegranate in modern art can be exemplified in the contrast between two very different paintings depicting the same subject, the goddess Persephone. The first is the work of the nineteenth-century poet-painter and founder of the Pre-Raphaelites Dante Gabriel Rossetti. In this work, Persephone has bitten from the pomegranate and realizes its consequences. In the diagonal centre of the piece is the fateful fruit, whose flesh is the colour of the goddess's lips. One of her hands supports the other, which holds its weight: that heavy balance of life and death. In contrast, a recent painting by Cha Davis represents Persephone in a most unusual way. It is part of a series in which Davis represents her pet chicken Ester in a number of different guises. The traditional form of a woman is abandoned, Persephone now taking on a new animal form. Rather than being held by her, pomegranates now sprout from the goddess-bird's head. The fruit, with their tentacle calyces, are identified as literally part of her body. These two artworks show the traditional and diverse ways individuals have approached representing the nature of the pomegranate in the Persephone myth. The fruit, with all its mystery and sensuality, is what makes these unique scenes. It is the pomegranate's simple yet aesthetically pleasing appearance that appeals and has remained such a seductive icon.

The Armenian Arts

The films of Sergei Parajanov are charged with pomegranate imagery, reflecting his Armenian heritage. In *Sayat-Nova* (The Colour of Pomegranates), the opening credits include a shot of juice spilling from pomegranates onto fabric, creating a stain in the shape of Armenia itself. Men in black robes are shown biting into pomegranates at a monastery. In the death scene of the poet protagonist we first see an ornamental dagger in the midst of several splattered pomegranates. A dreamlike sequence follows which features the poet having pomegranate juice (or is it blood?) poured on him by a white-faced woman wearing a green robe and a vegetal headdress (Death herself?). This draws on the long history of the pomegranate in Armenian art and architecture. The fruit appears on the thirteenth-century monastery of Geghard. A tympanum at one entrance is decorated with representations of trees from which hang entwined pomegranates and grape bunches. Two doves sit above the trees, looking inward towards the gateway. This pomegranate-grape-dove combination, all three of which represent life, is common in Armenian art. It appears

Cha Davis,
Ester Persephone,
2012.

among the mixture of biblical, mythological and rural-life-themed reliefs on the tenth-century Church of the Holy Cross at Akdamar Island. The pomegranate is also found as a column capital decoration at the seventh-century Zvartnots Cathedral. The fruit grows in the borders of pages from the Echmiadzin Gospel, a medieval Armenian illuminated bible from the tenth century. The longstanding fertility connotations of the pomegranate have resulted in the fruit's association with the Armenian wedding in modern times, pomegranate wine being the drink of choice for newlyweds. Armenians may wear a small dried pomegranate on a cord, known as a *taratosik*; this talismanic pendant is particularly associated with marriage.

In modern times the pomegranate has come to represent the resilience of the Armenian people during the genocide

Dante Gabriel Rossetti, *Prosperina* (the Roman name for the goddess). Rossetti has represented Persephone in a reflective pose, contemplating the effects of the fruit, 1874.

Church of the Holy Cross, Akdamar Island, 10th century.

A fallen pomegranate at the 7th-century Zvartnots Cathedral.

Illumination from the 10th-century Echmiadzin Gospel, Armenia.

of 1915. There is an Armenian saying that each pomegranate has 365 seeds, and that the people survived by eating one seed per day of their exile. The diaspora that resulted from the genocide saw the Armenian people spread across the world like the seeds of the pomegranate. The national importance of the fruit is honoured at the Armenian Genocide Monument of Larnaca, Cyprus, composed of a bronze sculpture surrounded by pomegranate and cypress trees. Armenian artists often use the pomegranate in their works to symbolize the suffering, hope, rebirth and survival that came with the genocide. Such an artist is the painter Rubik Kocharian, who was born in Armenia in 1940 and now lives in California. The pomegranate features in many of his works: being peeled by putti, split open in front of an Eastern lion relief, sitting next to a tablet inscribed with the Armenian alphabet, growing next to a classical sculpture. Kocharian's *Pomegranate Dance* demonstrates very traditional Armenian imagery, illustrating a dance between two women before a pomegranate-bearing statue.

Literature

The pomegranate has been used by many authors to emphasize an Eastern setting. This is the case for the pomegranate tree that plays a vital role in Khaled Hosseini's novel of sin and redemption, *The Kite Runner* (2003). The changes in the relationship between childhood friends Amir and Hassan are reflected in changes in the appearance of the pomegranate tree. The tree is introduced as their shelter, isolated from the rest of Kabul and the rest of the world. It is there that they climb, play, carve their names on its trunk and eat of its fruit. Most importantly, the plant becomes a kind of tree of knowledge, under which Amir reads and teaches the illiterate Hassan. Although Amir and Hassan are from different social classes, they become equal at the pomegranate tree. This is not to last. An atrocity happens. Hassan is raped, and although Amir witnesses the act, he lacks the courage to intervene. When they return later to the pomegranate tree it is not the same. Their paradise has been lost. Amir begins pelting pomegran-

Rubik Kocharian, *Pomegranate Dance*, 2010.

ates at Hassan, attempting to provoke him to fight back. The bloody imagery recalls the earlier rape scene:

> I hurled a pomegranate at him. It struck him in the chest, exploding in a spray of red pulp . . . I don't know how many times I hit him. All I know is that when I finally stopped, exhausted and panting, Hassan was smeared in red like he'd been shot by a firing squad.[1]

Amir wants to have his guilt lessened by being openly accused and punished for being the silent bystander. Instead, Hassan simply breaks a pomegranate over his own head. Throughout the rest of the novel Amir struggles for redemption. The pomegranate tree appears one more time, when Amir returns to Kabul much later as an adult. The tree no longer bears fruit. It has died, like his childhood friendship. All that remains is the memory of an idyllic time, embodied in those carvings made in the trunk long ago: 'Amir and Hassan, the sultans of Kabul.'[2]

The Armenian-American writer William Saroyan wrote a short story called 'The Pomegranate Trees' in which a certain Uncle Melik buys a plot of land in the desert and attempts to grow an oasis of pomegranates on it. The sceptical nephew narrator remarks: 'He was too imaginative and poetic for his own good. What he wanted was beauty. He wanted to plant it and see it grow . . . It was pure aesthetics, not agriculture.'[3] The trees are in constant battle with their environment, and get such little water they yield few fruit: 'My uncle harvested three small pomegranates. I ate one, he ate one, and we kept the other one up in his office.'[4] A year later two hundred pomegranates are harvested, which are packed into eleven boxes and sent to a produce man for selling. The fruit won't even sell at $1 a box, and are thus sent back to Melik and his nephew, who eat them. Melik, from lack of profit, is forced to sell the desert land back, but pleas that the trees still need to be looked after. He and his nephew come back to the spot three years later to find all the trees dead. The tale concludes with the poignant statement: 'we didn't say anything because there was such an awful lot to say, and no language to say it in.'[5] The pomegranate is instructional, functioning here as a symbol of the unattainable and unrealistic dream that will ultimately fail. It is the image of beauty, but not productivity. A similar perception is also found in Khalil Gibran's poem about the fruit, in which the author cannot bear the competing voices of the many seeds inside the pomegranate that he lives in, each expressing their hopes for the future. The parliament of seeds begin shouting their views simultaneously, becoming an indistinguishable noise. The author thus decides to move residence, to the quieter heart of a quince.

Painting and Sculpture

As we have seen, mankind has enthusiastically included the pomegranate in its portrayal of the world, both physical and transcendent, since the beginning of history. The modern era sees a continuation of this pattern, often in new ways. It is common to find Graeco-Roman and Renaissance sculptures holding the pomegranate. True innovation comes with Alexander Calder, pioneer of the hanging mobile, who in the 1940s created an abstract kinetic sculpture from aluminium sheeting, inspired by the pomegranate tree. A single suspended sheet-cut pomegranate gives meaning to the rest of the piece, allowing us to identify the freeform shapes that hang around it as leaves that form the tree. Through Calder, the classical pomegranate-bearing sculpture was resurrected and reimagined. Likewise, in modern still-life paintings of the pomegranate, popularly used in such compositions, we again see tribute paid to the fruit's symbolic position in ancient art. With its antique notions of death, the fruit often features as a vanitas symbol in still-life arrangements, reminding the viewer of his or her own mortality and the brevity of life (sometimes appearing alongside a skull or being cut by a knife).

Many notable modern artists have utilized the pomegranate in their own particular style: in Pablo Picasso's Cubism; in Henri Matisse's cut-outs; in the wallpapers of William Morris; in the glass lampshades of Louis Comfort Tiffany. The fruit plays a crucial role in the composition of Salvador Dalí's 1944 oil painting *Dream Caused by the Flight of a Bee around a Pomegranate a Second Before Awakening*. It illustrates a dream that was described to the artist by his wife Gala. This Surreal scene depicts two pomegranates. Gala's dream begins with a large broken-open pomegranate, two of its arils spilling out. From the fruit emerges a fish, from the fish emerges a tiger, and a second tiger emerges from the first. A rifle follows the tigers, the bayonet of which is about to pierce the naked body of Dalí's wife, which glows white in the centre of the scene. The pomegranate emphasizes the central theme of sexuality, the fruit being the original procreative force. Everything else emerges from its seeds in this Surrealist illustration of the Theory of Evolution. A second smaller pomegranate with a bee hovering around it gives the work its title. It casts a shadow in the shape of a heart. The fruit floats near Gala in recognition of the power of her female fertility. The pomegranate would also appear in later jewellery designed by Dalí. Rubies crafted to look like arils spill from his gold pomegranate heart brooch, with diamonds being used to represent the inner pith. In the ancient world, the pomegranate was a popular jewellery bead

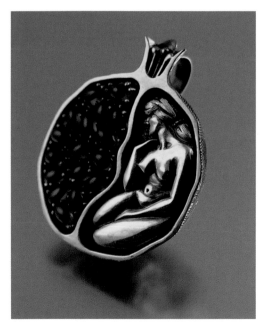

Silver pomegranate necklace with garnet crafted arils by Natalia Moroz and Sergey Zhiboedov of WingedLion. The naked figure evokes qualities of sensuality and femininity attributed to the pomegranate since ancient times.

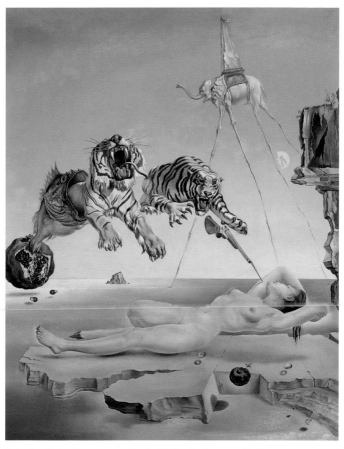

Salvador Dalí, *Dream Caused by the Flight of a Bee around a Pomegranate a Second Before Awakening,* 1944.

shape and, as Dalí's work demonstrates, it is still a fashionable ornament adorning brooches, necklaces, bracelets, rings and earrings today. The frequent use of garnet to represent the arils is appropriate in such jewellery, as this stone's name is derived from the Latin *granatum*, because of its similarity of colour to the pomegranate aril.

Ilya Zomb, *Fragment of Nightfall: Glimmer*, 2001.

Ilya Zomb, *Mutual Admiration to Pomegranates*, 2005.

Surrealist painters of today, following Dalí's example, continue to utilize the pomegranate in creating phantasmagorical worlds. Such an artist is Ilya Zomb, who has used the fruit in many of his works, particularly in association with ballerina figures who dance upon the giant fruits. Other paintings feature pomegranate seeds being pecked at by birds, or being strung together and formed into a necklace. Particularly potent in their representation of fertility are his works *Fragment of Nightfall: Glimmer* and *Mutual Admiration to Pomegranates*. In the former, two naked women recline against a giant pomegranate. Arils spill out, illuminating what is otherwise a dark and barren landscape (comparable to the underworld). Each of the women is holding and gazing into the large and luminous, jewel-like pomegranate seeds. *Mutual Admiration*, in contrast, features several regular-sized pomegranates. One pomegranate is being balanced on a ballerina's head, while another is impaled before her on the horn of a rhinoceros. Seeds drip down from the penetrated fruit. Four more pomegranates rest on a bench in the foreground.

One final artwork, a true masterpiece, brings together the recurring key themes of beauty, mystery and femaleness that we have seen accompany the fruit throughout this book. This is William-Adolphe Bouguereau's 1875 painting *L'Orientale à la grenade*, which features a young girl decked in oriental garb peeling a pomegranate with her hands. The girl, like the fruit she holds, represents Eastern beauty. The blood-red jewels of her earrings replicate the arils that she picks from her pomegranate. There is no contextual detail, the painting focusing solely on the desirable girl whose eyes gaze out of the right-hand side of the frame. The painting has a twin, *Marchande de grenades*. It depicts the same girl in the same outfit, only this time Bouguereau reveals her to be a pomegranate seller on the streets of Cairo (the medieval gate of Bab Zuweila visible in the background), sitting in the dust beside her basket of fruit. Her straight and piercing stare beseeches the viewer to purchase her pomegranates. As the pomegranate is so strongly linked with fertility, the vending of the fruit may represent a loss of virtue, making us question what she is really selling on the street.

Willem Kalf, *Still-life featuring Vanitas Motifs including a Pomegranate*, 1640s.

William-Adolphe Bouguereau, *Girl with a Pomegranate*, 1875.

Throughout this work I have illustrated, using the example of one food item, how people of the past made sense of what they were eating. Food is a language; its consumption makes a statement about who we are. In both the East and the West, gesture and story evolved around the pomegranate, adding to the experience of its consumption. The fruit was even imagined to accompany an individual's journey beyond the grave. It's not just the pomegranate's wonderful taste and health benefits that appeal to us today, but this ancient aesthetic that has stimulated the imagination since people partook of the pomegranate's delights for the first time.

Now it's time to take all that theory and put it into practice in the kitchen.

Appendix:
Pomegranate Cultivars

Cultivar Name(s)	Fruit Colour	Taste	Location of Origin
Agat	Red	Sweet-tart with soft seeds	Russia
Ahmar	Red	Sweet-tart	Iraq
Ak-Anar	Yellowish-white with red arils	Light	Turkey
Ambrosia	Pink fruit with purple arils	Sweet-tart	United States
Aswad	Purple-black	Sweet-tart	Iraq
Babylonian	Cream-green skin with white arils	Sweet-tart	Iraq
Balegal	Pale pink	Very sweet	United States
Blaze	Red	Tart	United States

Cagin	Red	Sour with hard seeds	Malta
Cloud	Greenish yellow fruit with pink blush, clear/white arils	Sweet	United States
Crab	Red	Sweet-tart	United States
Daru	Yellowish-green tinged with red, arils deep red to pinkish-white	Sour, used to make Anardana powder	India
Fleischman's	Pink	Very sweet	United States
Francis	Red	Sweet	Jamaica
Ganesh	Yellow-green to red in skin, pink arils	Sweet with soft seeds	India
Golden Globe	Yellow skin, red arils	Sweet	United States
Green Globe	Green	Sweet, very aromatic	United States
Home	Yellow-red fruit, pink arils	Sweet-tart	United States

Kandahar	Red, yellow or dark purple	Sweet, considered one of the best in the world	Afghanistan
Kizil Anar	Red	Sweet-tart	Turkey
Mollar	Red	Sweet	Spain
Nana	Red (ornamental variety often used as a hedge, although very small fruit are edible)	Sweet-tart	United States
Parfianka	Red	Soft and sweet-tart	Turkmenistan
Patras Acide	Red	Very sour	Greece
Patras Douce	Red	Sweet	Greece
Red silk	Dark pink	Sweet-tart	United States
Shahvar	Red	Sweet	Iran
Sin Pepe (means 'Seedless'). Also called Pink Ice or Pink Satin.	Red	Very sweet with soft seeds	United States

Sirenevyi	Pink skin, dark purple arils	Sweet with soft seeds	Turkmenistan
Sogdiana	Red	Complex sweet and tangy taste	Turkmenistan
Toryu-Shibori	Cream (ornamental dwarf variety grown mainly for its apricot-coloured flowers)	Tart	Japan
Wonderful	Purple-red	Sweet-tart, small medium-soft seeds	United States. The most commonly available variety in Western countries
Zaitiki	Red	Sweet with soft seeds	Cyprus

Recipes

Historical Recipes

Sausage on a Bed of Pomegranate and Grilled Plums

In the hilarious Roman mock epic the *Satyricon* (Chapter 31), we are told of a wealthy freedman named Trimalchio who arranges an extravagant banquet for guests at his home. One of the courses described is 'hot sausages, on a silver grill with sliced damson plums and pomegranate seeds underneath'. The effect of the fruit bears the likeness to flames, beneath the sausages. This is our only source for this dish, from which I have created a simple recipe based on the description. A beautiful mix of colours and flavours, it would work well as an entrée.

1 cup (1 fruit) pomegranate arils
6 plums, cut in halves
4 pork sausages (if you want to be really authentic, you can make your own ancient Roman Lucanian sausages, via the recipe provided in Dalby and Grainger's *The Classical Cookbook*)
melted butter or vegetable oil

Coat the plum halves in butter and grill on a barbecue until soft. Remove from heat and place in an oven to keep warm. Cook the sausages on a grill for about five to ten minutes until brown. When done, arrange the plums in rows on a platter. Scatter the pomegranate arils over the top. Cut the sausages into slices on the diagonal, and fan these over the top of the plums and pomegranate arils. Sprinkle with your choice of herbs and spices if desired.

Queen's Pottage
From John Nott's *The Cooks and Confectioners Dictionary* (London, 1723), recipe courtesy of Ivan Day at www.historicfood.com

This almond-flavoured soup, garnished with pomegranate, originates from medieval France, and can be found in La Varenne's 1651 cookbook *Le Cuisinier françois*. The dish came to enjoy popularity in England, and thus appears in an eighteenth-century English cookbook by John Nott. Alternate names for the dish include 'white soup' (the one frequently consumed by Jane Austen characters) and 'hedgehog soup' (it was sometimes served with small rolls spiked with almonds, giving the appearance of the animal). The earliest recipe, La Varenne's, instructs the chef to toast the surface of the soup with a red-hot fire shovel.

Beat Almonds, and boil them in good Broth, a few Crums of Bread, the Inside of a Lemon, and a Bunch of sweet Herbs, stir them often, strain them, then soak Bread in the best Broth, which is to be thus made; Bone a Capon or Partridge, pownd the Bones in a Mortar, then boil them in strong Broth, with Mushrooms, then strain them through a Linnencloth; with this Broth soak your Bread; as it soaks, sprinkle it with the Almond-broth. Then put a little minced Meat to it, either of Partridge or Capon, and still as it is soaking, put in more Almond-broth, until it be full, then hold a red-hot iron over it; garnish the Dish with Pomegranates, Pistaches, and Cocks-combs.

Royal Salad

From Antonio Latini, *Lo scalco moderna* (Naples, 1692 and 1694), recipe courtesy of Ivan Day at www.historicfood.com

Crunchy and fruity, the pomegranate does well in any salad. The popularity the pomegranate enjoys in the salad today is not a new phenomenon, however. A salad recipe from the seventh-century cookbook *Le Cuisinier méthodique* consisted simply of pomegranate arils, lemon slices and pistachios, sprinkled with sugar.

Take endive, or scarola (another species of endive or chicory), mince it finely and put it to one side, until you have prepared a large basin, at the bottom of which are eight or ten biscottini, friselle or taralli (all three are types of hard breads), soaked in water and vinegar, with a little white salt. Put the said chopped endive on top, intermix with other salad stuff, albeit minced finely, make the body of the said salad on top at your discretion, intermix with radishes cut into pieces lengthways, filling in the gaps in the said basin with the ingredients listed below, all arranged in order. Pine nuts four ounces, stoned olives six ounces, capers four ounces, one pomegranate, white and black grapes ten ounces, twelve anchovies, tarantello (salted belly of tuna) four ounces, botargo three ounces, comfits, six ounces, preserved citron (and) preserved pumpkin twelve ounces, four hard-boiled eggs, whole pistachios four ounces, four ounces of raisins, other black olives six ounces. Caviar, four ounces, minced flesh of white fish, six ounces, little radishes, salt, oil and vinegar to taste, garnish the plate with slices of citrons, and citron flowers round about in order, take heed not to add salt or seasonings, until it goes to the table, and is about to be eaten.

Granada Salad

From *Los Angeles Times Cook Book,* No. 21 (1905), submitted
by S. Miller of 454 North Fair Oaks Avenue, Pasadena, California.
A digital version of this cookbook is accessible
online at http://digital.lib.msu.edu

Place the fruit (pomegranate) in the ice box until cold. Cut open
with a sharp knife across the fruit division. Scrape out the red
particles with a silver spoon. Place on shredded lettuce hearts
and serve with the following salad dressing: Yolks of six eggs,
one teaspoon mustard, one teaspoon salt, six teaspoons sugar,
half cup of vinegar, half cup rich milk, one tablespoon butter
and dash of cayenne pepper. Beat yolks, mustard, salt and sugar
together; add vinegar and milk; then remaining ingredients. Cook
in double boiler until thick. A cup of whipped cream added just
before serving improves this dressing.

Modern Recipes

Güllaç

Recipe courtesy of Zerrin Gunaydin at www.giverecipe.com

The pomegranate plays an important role in Middle Eastern
sweets. The Turkish confection *güllaç* is considered the forerunner
from which baklava originates. It consists of thin layers of white
pastry soaked in sweetened milk and rosewater. Between the layers
are placed chopped walnuts, and a garnish of pistachio and pomegranate arils on top adds colour to the dessert. The dish originates
from the Ottoman period, dating as far back as the fourteenth
century, and is described in the Chinese food and health manual
the *Yinshan Zhenyao*. It is especially popular during Ramadan, as it
is light on the stomach after a full day's fasting. This dish relies on
access to *güllaç* wafers, which may be difficult to access in Western
countries but should be available in Middle Eastern grocers.

10 *güllaç* sheets
6 cups (1½ litres) milk
1¾ cup (350 g) sugar
1 cup (150 g) finely chopped walnuts
rosewater (optional)
pomegranate arils and finely chopped pistachio for garnishing

Put milk and sugar (and 1 tablespoon rosewater if you like) in a saucepan and apply heat until the sugar dissolves. Stir it occasionally and make sure it does not boil. Allow to cool; if you use the milk hot, your dessert will become mushy.

Lay your first *güllaç* sheet in a square dish. Wet it with the warm milk. Repeat this with five sheets. Spread the crumbled walnut on the fifth. Then, lay another five sheets on top one by one, wetting each of them with milk. When you finish with the tenth one, pour the rest of the milk over the top. As the layers will combine when they are wet with the milk, they don't need to be perfectly arranged. After pouring the milk, the sheets will rise, but do not touch them. Cover the dish with plastic wrap and put it in the refrigerator for at least two hours. Leave the garnishing to just before you serve the dish, otherwise pomegranates and pistachio may change its colour. When you are ready to eat your *güllaç*, remove it from the refrigerator, cut it into squares, garnish and serve.

Pomegranate Cobbler

The cobbler was created early on by settlers in American colonies. Depending on the region, the crust can be the consistency either of crisp biscuit or soft cake, and may be placed either above or below the fruit. Almost any fruit can be used as the base for this popular dessert, and the pomegranate is no exception.

3 cups (2–3 fruit) pomegranate arils
½ cup (100 g) caster sugar for fruit, and ¾ cup (150 g)
caster sugar for batter

1 teaspoon baking powder
1 cup (115 g) plain flour
1 egg
½ cup (125 ml) milk
1 tsp vanilla extract
¼ cup (60 ml) melted butter

Sift flour, baking powder and ¾ cup (150 g) of the sugar into a bowl. Add the vanilla, milk, egg and melted butter, and beat the mixture on high for about 5 minutes until a smooth consistency is achieved. In a baking dish, stir pomegranate arils and the ½ cup (100 g) sugar together. Pour the batter in an even layer over the fruit. Bake for 45 minutes at 180°C (360°F) or until the top is golden brown and springs back. Serve hot with vanilla ice cream.

Grenadine

Grenadine, a syrup made from the pomegranate, is very simple to make and is very useful. Today, most store-bought grenadine is artificially produced and contains no pomegranate. Grenadine is a common finishing ingredient in many classic cocktails including the Singapore Sling, Shirley Temple, Roy Rogers, Tequila Sunrise, Mimosa and Purple Rain. In mixology, the syrup is fairly interchangeable with fresh pomegranate juice or pomegranate liqueur, all three of which make an effective addition to a glass of champagne. Pomegranate is becoming a common addition in creating new takes on cocktail classics like Martinis, Cosmopolitans and Daiquiris. A much thicker version of grenadine, known in Middle Eastern cuisine as *nasharab*, is served as a sauce on fish and meat.

juice of 2 pomegranates (500 ml)
1 cup (200 g) sugar

Pour pomegranate juice and sugar into a small saucepan. Place on a medium heat on your stovetop. Allow sugar to dissolve and liquid to boil for about 10 minutes (or longer if you want a thicker sauce).

A dash of lemon may be added for additional tartness if desired. Refrigerate in container before use.

Chocolate Pomegranate Drops

1 200-g (8-oz) bar milk or dark chocolate
1 cup (1 fruit) pomegranate arils

Melt the chocolate and stir in the pomegranate arils. Spoon portions onto baking paper or into patty pans, and allow to set in a refrigerator. A very simple yet delicious treat. Nuts, coconut and marshmallow can be added to create a pomegranate Rocky Road.

Kolliva
Recipe courtesy of Maria Benardis, from her book *My Greek Family Table* (Sydney, 2009).

This traditional Greek dish, prepared following the death of a loved one, preserves the antique notion of the pomegranate as a memorial food item.

4 cups (500 g) wheat kernels
2 tsp ground cinnamon, plus extra, for decorating
1 ⅔ cup (250 g) walnuts, chopped
½ cup (75 g) raisins
2 cups (250 g) sesame seeds, toasted and crushed
½ cup (60 g) icing sugar, sifted
½ cup (75 g) blanched almonds, halved
arils of 1 pomegranate

Cover the wheat kernels with water and soak overnight. Drain and rinse well.

Fill saucepan with water, add the soaked wheat and bring to a rapid boil. Reduce the heat and simmer for two hours until the wheat is tender and begins to split open. Stir frequently to prevent sticking, and add more water as required. When the wheat is cooked, remove the pan from the heat and leave to stand for about thirty minutes. Drain the wheat and rinse thoroughly in a colander. Spread it out on a clean tea towel and leave for about two hours, shaking occasionally. Place in a bowl, add the cinnamon, walnuts, raisins and half the sesame seeds and mix gently. Press the mixture down hard on a serving platter and spread the remaining sesame seeds evenly over the top. Dust with a thin layer of icing sugar. Sprinkle the cinnamon to form a cross on the *kolliva*, then place the almonds on either side of the cinnamon to cross the cross. Place the pomegranate seeds over the exposed icing sugar to form a colourful design. To serve, simply spoon some of the mixture into small bowls. Serve at room temperature.

Pomegranate Macarons
The star of the pomegranate macaron lies in the fruity ganache filling, sandwiched between two almond macarons.
This recipe is contributed by blogger Barbara Chung
of www.themacarondiaries.tumblr.com

For the pomegranate ganache filling:
¼ cup (60 ml) thickened cream
juice of 1 pomegranate (yields about ¼ cup (50 ml))
1 cup (130 g) white chocolate, chopped

Chop up the white chocolate and put aside. Cut the pomegranate in half and, with great force, squeeze the juice out into a bowl. Allow the seeds to fall into the bowl as well. Pick out the extra seeds that don't easily fall in with a spoon and add them to the bowl. Pour the squeezed juice through a strainer into another bowl. Using a spoon, push the seeds into the strainer to extract as much juice as you can. Set aside.

In a small saucepan, on low heat, bring the cream to boil and remove from heat. Pour the hot cream over the chopped chocolate and mix until the chocolate has completely blended with the cream. Once the white chocolate and cream mixture has cooled, stir through the freshly squeezed pomegranate juice. Keep the mixture covered and refrigerate overnight.

For the macarons:
1¼ cups (135 g) almond meal (ground almonds)
1½ cups (180 g) confectioners' (icing) sugar
3 large egg whites aged at room temperature for a minimum of 24 hours
5 tablespoons (65 g) caster sugar
½ tablespoon red powdered food colouring

Combine the ground almonds with the icing sugar and red powdered macaron colouring and sift three times (or process the almonds and sugar in a food processor if you have one). Set aside. Beat the egg whites until foamy and then add the caster sugar one tablespoon at a time until mixture is thick, shiny and stiff. Fold in half of the dry mixture with the egg whites until combined. Then add about 80 per cent of the rest of the mixture (this is to make sure that the batter doesn't end up being too dry) and mix lightly in a circular motion. Commence folding the macaron mixture until it moves slowly when the bowl is rocked from side to side. A good way to check is by scooping a spoonful of batter and let it drop back into the bowl. If it slowly drops back into the bowl, lands on the rest of the batter in a small mound and slowly sinks back into the batter, then the process is complete. Do not over-fold your batter as this may cause your macaron batter to become overly runny and, consequently, have no feet.

Line trays with double layers of baking paper. The double layer helps to prevent heat from passing through too quickly. Scoop the macaron mixture into a piping bag and pipe small mounds of macaron batter (about 2–2.5 cm or 1 inch diameter) onto the lined trays. Once you are done, tap the tray firmly against the counter or other flat surface to release any trapped air from the piped shells. This will help the macarons hold their round shape and enables the *pieds* or little 'feet' to form. Set aside the trays to dry at room temperature. In order for macarons to form a smooth, shiny dome, the batter must not stick to your finger when touched.

Once the batter is dried, you may place them into the oven. Bake at 120–130°C (250–265°F) for 15–20 minutes; it is best to keep your eye on the macarons as each oven differs. Once you take them out of the oven, place the tray on a cooling rack and allow the shells to cool. Once the macarons have cooled, you may sandwich the shells with the pomegranate ganache filling to complete your macaron. Rest the macarons in the fridge overnight in order for the shells to absorb the moisture from the filling. Serve the completed macarons at room temperature.

References

Introduction

1 David Zohary, with Maria Hopf and Ehud Weiss, *Domestication of Plants in the Old World: The Origin and Spread of Domesticated Plants in Southwest Asia, Europe, and the Mediterranean Basin* (Oxford, 2013), pp. 134–5.
2 John M. Riddle, *Goddesses, Elixirs, and Witches: Plants and Sexuality throughout Human History* (New York, 2010), p. 17.
3 Such as at Jericho. Other Bronze Age sites have yielded dried pomegranate fruit being used as cups or boxes themselves. Charles Singer, ed., *A History of Technology*, vol. I: *From Early Times to Fall of Ancient Empires* (Oxford, 1990), p. 372.

1 The Primordial Pomegranate: The Fruit in Myth

1 Efthymios G. Lazongas, 'Personification in Myth and Cult: Side, the Personification of the Pomegranate', in *Personification in the Greek World*, ed. Emma J. Stafford and Judith Herrin (Farnham, 2005), p. 104.
2 As described in one of the few surviving fragments of Heliodorus' extensive fifteen-book work on the Athenian Acropolis.

3 Pausanias, *Description of Greece*: 2.17.4, trans. W.H.S. Jones
   (Cambridge, MA, 1918), p. 335.
4 Helmut Kyrieleis, 'The Heraion at Samos', in *Greek
   Sanctuaries: New Approaches* (London, 1995), p. 106.
5 Aeschylus, *Eumenides*, 657–63.
6 Or in some versions compared to the pomegranate as in
   Ovid, *Metamorphoses*, 10.734–8.
7 Clement of Alexandria, *Exhortation to the Greeks*, 2.15, trans.
   G. W. Butterworth (Cambridge, MA, 1919), p. 177.
8 The Golden Apple of Discord is one of the fruit from
   the Garden of the Hesperides, which were fabled to grant
   immortality. In the myth of Atalanta another golden 'apple'
   leads to sexual conquest.
9 Powys Mathers, *The Book of the Thousand Nights and One
   Night*, vol. III (London and New York, 2005), p. 301.
10 Ibid., p. 401.
11 Shahnameh 1.21–3.
12 Ignacz Kunos, *Forty-four Turkish Fairy Tales* (London, 1913),
   p. 171.
13 Ibid.
14 Ibid., p. 172.
15 Reader's Digest, *Timeless Tales from Many Lands* (New York,
   2001), p. 330.
16 Homa A. Ghahremani, 'Simorgh: An Old Persian Fairy
   Tale', *Sunrise Magazine* (June/July 1984).

2 Pomegranates in the Ancient World

1 Jean Bottéro, *The Oldest Cuisine in the World: Cooking in
   Mesopotamia*, trans. Teresa Lavender Fagan (Chicago, IL,
   2004), pp. 101–2.
2 Samuel Kramer, *The Sacred Marriage Rite: Aspects of Faith,
   Myth, and Ritual in Ancient Sumer* (Bloomington, IN, 1969),
   p. 100.
3 Sidney Smith, 'Pomegranate as a Charm', *Man*, XXV (1925),
   p. 142.

4 John M. Riddle, *Goddesses, Elixirs, and Witches: Plants and Sexuality throughout Human History* (New York, 2010), p. 20.

5 Sara Immerwahr, 'The Pomegranate Vase: Its Origins and Continuity', *Hesperia*, LVIII/4 (1989), p. 408.

6 Pausanias, 9.25.1

7 Philostratus, *Images*, 2.29.

8 Nikolaos Kaltsas, *Sculpture in the National Archaeological Museum, Athens* (Los Angeles, CA, 2002), p. 48.

9 Philostatus, *Vita Apollonii*, 4.28.

10 *Odyssey,* 7.113.

11 Herodotus 7.41.

12 Herodotus 4.143.

13 Plutarch, *The Parallel Lives: Artaxerxes*, 4.3, trans Bernadotte Perrin (Cambridge, MA, 1923), p. 135.

14 Pliny, *Natural History*, 13.2, 20.82, 21.84, 22.70, 23.16, 23.42, 23.43, 23.57, 23.58, 23.60, 24.54, 29.11, 30.16.

15 Found in the Byzantine book of court protocol the *De Ceremoniis*. Cited in Kathryn M. Ringrose, 'Women and Power at the Byzantine Court', in *Servants of the Dynasty: Palace Women in World History*, ed. Anne Walthall (Berkeley, CA, 2008), p. 77.

16 Efthymios G. Lazongas, 'Personification in Myth and Cult: Side, the Personification of the Pomegranate', in *Personification in the Greek World*, ed. Emma J. Stafford and Judith Herrin (Farnham, 2005), p. 102.

3 Jewish and Islamic Pomegranates

1 Asaph Goor, 'The History of the Pomegranate in the Holy Land', *Economic Botany*, XXI/3 (1967), pp. 221–2.

2 Ibid., p. 223.

3 As exemplified in Joel 1:10, 12.

4 Hebrew for 'pomegranate'.

5 Goor, 'The History of the Pomegranate in the Holy Land', p. 222.

6 Ibid., p. 223.

7 Mary Abram, 'The Pomegranate: Sacred, Secular, and Sensuous Symbol of Ancient Israel', *Studia Antiqua*, VII/1 (Spring 2009), p. 27.

8 Kiddushin 81b.

9 Abu Nu'aim, *As-Suyuti's Medicine of the Prophet* (Bloomington, IN, 1994), p. 63.

4 Medieval Pomegranates

1 Melitta Weiss Adamson, *Food in Medieval Times* (Westport, CT, 2004), pp. 113–14.

2 Pliny, *Natural History*, 23.58.

3 Christopher Daniell, *Death and Burial in Medieval England, 1066–1550* (London, 1997), p. 76.

4 Henry Layard, *A Popular Account of Discoveries at Nineveh* (New York, 1854), p. 302.

5 A local tradition of Andalusia.

6 Bury Palliser, *Historic Devices, Badges, and War-cries* (London, 1870), p. 380.

7 Hildegard Schneider, 'On the Pomegranate', *Metropolitan Museum of Art Bulletin*, IV/4 (1945), p. 118.

8 Monica H. Green, *The Trotula: A Medieval Compendium of Women's Medicine* (Philadelphia, PA, 2001), pp. 87, 97 and 171.

5 Pomegranate Production and Culture Today

1 Peter Collinson and William Darlington, *Memorials of John Bartram and Humphry Marshall* (Philadelphia, PA, 1849), p. 244.

2 Note that many modern takes on grenadine substitute the pomegranate juice for artificial flavouring.

3 Richard Ashton, with Barbara Baer and David Silverstein, eds, *The Incredible Pomegranate* (Tempe, AZ, 2006), p. 76.

4 Ben Farmer, 'Afghanistan Promotes Pomegranates over Opium Poppies in Farming Overhaul', *The Telegraph* (20 November 2008).

5 Julia Morton, *Fruit of Warm Climates* (Miami, FL, 1987), pp. 352–5.

6 Ashton, Baer and Silverstein, eds, *The Incredible Pomegranate*, p. 21.

7 Gregory Levin, *Pomegranate Roads: A Soviet Botanist's Exile from Eden* (Forestville, CA, 2006), p. 25.

8 Ibid., pp. 147–8.

9 Ibid., p. 180.

10 Ibid., p. 101.

11 John M. Riddle, *Goddesses, Elixirs, and Witches: Plants and Sexuality throughout Human History* (New York, 2010), p. 18.

12 Ibid.

13 Ibid.

14 Ibid., p. 50.

15 Donald Harper, 'Flowers in T'ang Poetry: Pomegranate, Sea Pomegranate, and Mountain Pomegranate', *Journal of American Oriental Studies*, CVI/1 (1986), p. 152.

16 Sri Sathya Sai Baba, 'True Sacrifice', at http://sssbpt.org/index.html, July 1988.

17 Kabir Edmund Helminski, *Love's Ripening: Rumi on the Heart's Journey* (Boston, MA, 2008), pp. 56–7.

18 *Macquarie Dictionary* (revised 3rd edn), p. 1478.

6 The Pomegranate in Modern Literature, Art and Film

1 Khaled Hosseini, *The Kite Runner* (London, 2003), pp. 80–81.

2 Ibid., p. 24.

3 William Sayoran, *My Name is Aram* (San Diego, CA, 1940), p. 27.

4 Ibid., p. 39.

5 Ibid., p. 42.

Select Bibliography

Abram, Mary, 'The Pomegranate: Sacred, Secular, and Sensuous Symbol of Ancient Israel', *Studia antiqua*, VII/1 (2009)

Ashton, Richard, with Barbara Baer and David Silverstein, eds, *The Incredible Pomegranate* (Tempe, AZ, 2006)

Goor, Asaph, 'The History of the Pomegranate in The Holy Land', *Economic Botany*, XXI/3 (1967)

Immerwahr, Sara, 'The Pomegranate Vase: Its Origins and Continuity', *Hesperia*, LVIII/4 (1989)

Lazongas, Efthymios G., 'Personification in Myth and Cult: Side, the Personification of the Pomegranate', in *Personification in the Greek World*, ed. Emma Stafford and Judith Herrin (Farnham, 2005)

Levin, Gregory, *Pomegranate Roads: A Soviet Botanist's Exile from Eden* (Forestville, CA, 2006)

Muthmann, Friedrich, *Der Granatapfel* (Bern, 1982)

Riddle, John M., *Goddesses, Elixirs, and Witches: Plants and Sexuality Throughout Human History* (New York, 2010)

Seeram, Navindra P., with Risa N. Schulman and David Heber, eds, *Pomegranates: Ancient Roots to Modern Medicine* (Boca Raton, FL, 2006)

Websites and Associations

A very informative website on pomegranates put out by the
University of Florida
www.crec.ifas.ufl.edu/extension/pomegranates

Aril Systems
Promotional website of a pomegranate seed-extractor machine
www.arilsystem.com

Pom Wonderful
Leading American distributor
www.pomwonderful.com

Pomlife
Australian distributor
www.pomlife.com.au

Website of the Pomegranate Council. Notable are pages on
crafts (make your own pomegranate wreath!) and recipes
www.pomegranates.org

Acknowledgements

This book is dedicated to my mother, who always gave me books and took me to museums. Writing it wouldn't have been possible without the help and support of many people. A big thanks to editor Andy Smith, and everyone at Reaktion Books for being most helpful throughout this project. Many thanks to all of my family and friends who listened politely and made suggestions, while I rambled on about pomegranates. Of note are the contributions of Clementine Sugita, Wendy Stone, Geoffrey Page, Louise Pryke and Beatrice McLoughlin. A special thanks goes to Rebecca Psarras for pointing me in the direction of (and helping me consume) a variety of pomegranate products.

Thank you to the artists and museums who have allowed use of their images throughout this work. Gratitude is also due to recipe contributors Barbara Chung, Maria Benardis, Ivan Day and Zerrin Gunaydin.

Photo Acknowledgements

The author and the publishers wish to express their thanks to the below sources of illustrative material and/or permission to reproduce it.

Alamy: p. 35 (The Print Collector); Suky Best: p. 77; © The Trustees of The British Museum, London: pp. 28, 31 bottom, 34, 43, 44, 45, 50, 65; Brooklyn Museum of Art, New York: p. 31 top right; Corbis: pp. 8 (ImageBROKER), 11 (Guenter Rossenbach), 12 (Steve Goossen), 46 (Mimmo Jodice), 66 (Summerfield Press), 108 (Cha Davis), 109 (Christie's Images), 117 (Museo Thyssen-Bornemisza, Madrid © Salvador Dalí, Fundació Gala-Salvador Dalí, DACS); Flickr: p. 110 bottom; Dumbarton Oaks Collection, Washington, DC: p. 51; Getty Images: p. 47 (Leemage); J. P. Getty Museum/The Getty, Los Angeles: p. 120; Homonihilis: p. 18; iStockphoto: p. 6 (Emrah Turudu); Jebulon: pp. 72, 74, 75, 80; Kasir: p. 101 bottom; Rubik Kocharian: p. 113; Los Angeles County Museum of Art: p. 96; The Louvre Museum, Paris: pp. 42, 59, 61; Itzhak Luvation: p. 55; Aren Maerir: p. 40; Urek Meniashvili: p. 99; The Metropolitan Museum of Art, New York: pp. 21, 36 top, 39, 60, 62, 68; Moonsun1981: p. 100; Natalia Moroz and Sergey Zhiboedov: p. 116; Ruslan Sergeev: p. 101 top; Spoliast: p. 71; Tokyo National Museum: p. 95; Victoria & Albert Museum, London: p. 104; The Walters Art Gallery, Baltimore: pp. 36 bottom, 67, 92; Werner Forman Archive: p. 32 (The Louvre

Index

italic numbers refer to illustrations; **bold** to recipes